The New European Landscape

Michael Lancaster

Butterworth Architecture
An imprint of Butterworth-Heineman Ltd
Linacre House, Jordan Hill, Oxford OX2 8DP

 A member of the Reed Elsevier group

OXFORD   LONDON   BOSTON
MUNICH   NEW DELHI   SINGAPORE   SYDNEY
TOKYO   TORONTO   WELLINGTON

First published 1994

British Library Cataloguing in Publication Data
Lancaster, Michael
    New European Landscape
    I. Title
    712.094

ISBN 0 7506 1546 X

Library of Congress Cataloguing in Publication Data
A catalogue record for this book is available from the
Library of Congress

Composition by Scribe Design, Gillingham, Kent
Printed in Great Britain

The New European Landscape

To Renate, June, Stephen and Julian

Contents

Preface

The idea for this book grew out of a discussion between myself and two colleagues, Robert Holden and Tom Turner. It was to celebrate the formation of the European Community with the aid of sponsorship by various official and commercial organizations. While the sponsorship failed to materialize, the cause for celebration was overwhelmed by events and I found myself looking optimistically towards a much wider Europe than originally envisaged. Instead of the original twelve, I made approaches to twenty-five countries on the basis of information supplied by another colleague, Roger Seijo, through the European landscape education network, ELEE. The representatives, whom I describe as Contributors, were each requested to send brief introductory notes on the state of landscape education, the development of the profession and a selection of examples of work which could be regarded as typical. The aim was to produce a book that would be representative of landscape architecture over the last few decades in a geographical Europe extending from the Atlantic to the Urals.

Inevitably, the aim had to be modified. Continuing political changes, poor communications, and the variety of work submitted, have resulted firstly in a reduction in the number of countries, and secondly in a need to restructure the book according to subject areas. This, I believe, has distinct advantages when dealing with the work of such a young profession. A consequence is that the material supplied and the introductions for different countries have not, in general, been treated separately. Exceptions occur where this is consistent with the subject layout. I am extremely grateful to the contributors for generously accepting these modifications; also for their patience.

Because of the difficulties of illustrating them effectively, I have omitted landscape planning projects and those principally concerned with ecology and conservation, industrial and mineral workings, roads and other forms of transport – although these are obviously important aspects of landscape design. Limited space has also compelled me to exclude most projects concerned with historical conservation and housing, the latter deserving a book of its own. In giving credits for example, I have concentrated primarily, where possible, on individual designers and secondly on practices. Also I have avoided listing large numbers of names associated with client bodies and other institutions.

In view of the changes, I have taken it upon myself to broaden the field of enquiry beyond my original brief on 'what is happening in Europe?', to develop a number of ideas that have been germinating in my mind since the late 1960s when I began to teach Landscape Architecture in a School of Architecture, Landscape and Planning. Having begun my career in architecture and, in a sense, moved beyond it, I have been conscious of an uneasy relationship between the environmental disciplines which persists in many countries. There are obvious reasons for this professional jealousy between the only two *design* professions directly charged with the design of the environment – one of which has great numerical superiority. But there are other, more profound reasons arising from the nature of the work and difficulties of communication between the disciplines themselves, as well as with the general public. This applies even more to the scientific languages used by structural and civil engineers on the one hand and biologists and land scientists on the other, all of whom have an important influence on the environment. Architecture is at least unequivocal in its concern with buildings; Landscape Architecture spreads out in an ungainly fashion from the 'built' to the 'natural' environment (the meaning of environment itself is questionable).

In the first part of the book, 'Connections', I have attempted to address the problem of definitions and usages, which allows such gaps in understanding to occur. I refer to the cultural gap between the arts and sciences and the question of taste. In addition I have addressed the problem of the environment and how we experience it, of nature and ecology, and their links with art and design. Lastly, I have written a brief historical summary of landscape architecture as a profession. Although I have used information supplied by contributors and referred to documented sources, this is my own interpretation, and I must stress the need to refer to the relevant institutions for up-to-date information in such a changing field.

I have divided the examples with their descriptive texts – which comprise the bulk of the work submitted by contributors – into three parts which I call: 'Nature rediscovered', 'Landscape and the city', and 'Landscapes of memory'. They are not mutually exclusive: landscape architecture by its nature being non-specialized. But it was a convenient way of grouping examples according to my choice of priorities: that is, the messages I wished to convey. Thus Part 2 begins with nature in its most natural form and ends with nature at its most artificial – albeit still nature. Many of the examples are also urban; but they are, perhaps, less typically urban than those that I have gathered together in Part 3. In this part I have stressed the importance of open spaces of all kinds which characterize towns and cities. These include major natural open spaces, public parks and gardens, playgrounds, civic squares and shopping streets, which in the past have often been considered separately, but which we are now beginning to appreciate collectively as parts of integrated systems in which we spend much of our lives. Finally Part 4, 'Landscapes of memory', includes those landscapes that have an obvious resonance arising from their association with religion, death, history and art, all of which are closely connected.

Although colour is an important aspect of all landscapes, I have taken the view that many can more appropriately be illustrated in black and white because of the accentuation of contrasts. With this in mind, I have grouped the colour illustrations into two sections, each carrying a message that must be expressed in colour. The first deals with 'natural' colour in the sense that the medium is natural, being in the form of plants or natural building materials. The second deals with colour reflected by artificial surfaces in the context of the landscape. It is very much a current problem, arising from the number of large buildings which are now perceived to intrude, inviting creative solutions in terms of their relationship with the landscape.

Acknowledgements

I am grateful to Charles Jencks and Herbert Gans for material referred to in Section 1.1, to Peter Stevens and his publishers, Little, Brown & Co and Penguin Books, and Stefan Bartha for some of the ideas and material referred to in Section 1.4, and the University of Greenwich (formerly Thames Polytechnic) for material in the introductory chapters, which I was able to explore in my lecture course Aspects of Design. I wish to thank many friends and colleagues, in particular: Patrick Goode, Robert Holden and Tom Turner for their help and advice in relating to the structure and content also for the use of published material by them on the subjects of public parks and new developments in France and Spain; Sarah Zarmati for work on French parks; Lorzing on the development of the park in Holland; Carol Jones, Peter Hayden (the CIS) and Uli Seitz (Stuttgart) for help on specific items; Roger Seijo for assisting with contributors and providing information on education and practice in various European countries; and, of course, the contributors for their generosity and hard work in writing and assembling material. The individual texts for Spanish contributions are by: M.N. Bedoya, S.M. Cuellar, M.S. Brodsky and A.S. Alcaráz. In two cases the work was translated: from the Spanish by Beatrix Garcia Figueras and from the Italian by Clare Littlewood. In addition I should like to thank those other contributors whom I approached directly, particularly those who provided material relating to Britain, these include Brian Carter, Neil Higson, Edward Hutchinson and Hal Moggridge. Also I wish to thank my publisher, Neil Warnock-Smith, and his colleagues for their forbearance.

Contributors

The CIS	**Elena Mikoulina** Professor; Architectural Institute, Moscow
Belgium	**Jef de Gryse** Landscape Architect; Visiting Professor at various schools of landscape architecture
Denmark	**Jette Abel** Associate Professor in Landscape Architecture. Royal Veterinary and Agricultural University, Copenhagen
	Karen Attwell Associate Professor in Landscape Architecture, Royal Veterinary and Agricultural University, Copenhagen
Finland	**Tuula-Maria Merivuori** Landscape Architect, Planning Office, City of Espoo; Acting Professor in Landscape Architecture, University of Technology, Helsinki
France	**Christophe Girot** Professor, School of Landscape Architecture, Versailles, France; Visiting Professor, Harvard School of Design
Germany	**Frieder Luz** Landscape Architect; Professor Fachhochschule, Weihenstephan
Greece	**Anastasia Remundu-Triantafyllis** Architect/Town Planner, Ministry of Regional Planning and Environment
Italy	**Biagio Guccione** Architect/Landscape Architect; Visiting Professor, Genoa University; Reader in Landscape Architecture; University of Florence

Luxembourg	**John Weier de Haas** Landscape Architect
The Netherlands	**Michiel den Ruijter** Landscape Architect; Professor of Landscape Architecture, International Agricultural College, Larenstein
Slovenia	**Ina Šukle** Lecturer in Landscape Architecture, Faculty of Biotechnology, University Edvarda Kardelja, Ljubljana
Spain	**Carmen Añon** Professor, School of Architecture, Polytechnic University, Madrid
Switzerland	**Heiner Rodel** Landscape Architect
Turkey	**Yalçin Özgen** Professor, Department of Landscape Architecture, Faculty of Forestry, University of Istanbul

Introduction

There is a deliberate ambiguity in the title. The New European Landscape applies both to the new *designed* landscapes, which are the main theme of the book, and to the landscape context with which I am principally concerned in the introductory chapters. The former category includes examples that have been designed mainly for public use and visual effect. The latter includes everything else that makes up our habitat, and which we now call the environment. It is the product of centuries of development of all kinds, from the natural to the cultivated, the urban, the suburban, the industrial and the derelict. For generations we have been inclined to separate these categories. Our retreat from the land has encouraged a reductionist mode of thought which effectively divides them, not only from one another, but from nature, which is often regarded as some sort of fine weather luxury connected with wild life. But as the century rushes towards completion, we are being forced to realize how all things are connected. Our personal surroundings – the familiar landscape/townscape – can no longer be considered in isolation. *The Everywhere Landscape* (Brown, 1982) is all one: each part impinges on all the other parts which together make up our environment. This is the new enlightenment.

Even the idea of landscape is elusive. It ranges between nature and culture, the organic and the inorganic, between the horticultural and the architectural, the natural and the built, the soft and the hard, the curved and the straight, from the timeless to the immediate and from the very large to the very small. We are conditioned to *see* it and to judge it in painted or photographic images; we *experience* it as space enclosed or punctuated by buildings, trees and shaped land. Coupled with architecture, the landscape becomes both focus and setting, subjected to those criteria by which we judge design – space and form, colour and texture, function and durability.

The relationship with nature is equivocal. Both architecture and landscape begin with habitat. The Old German *Landschaft* included the dwelling, outbuildings, cultivated land, surrounding forest and common grazing land, animals, people, and their mutual obligation (Stilgoe, 1982). The old English form referred to a district or tract of country, and it re-entered the language in the sixteenth century from the Dutch *Landscap*, an artists' term for 'a picture representing inland scenery' (*Oxford English Dictionary*). Landscape painting was then understood as an art which selected the best of nature, improving and perfecting it where appropriate; a technique that was applied directly to the land by the English garden designers of the eighteenth century: 'I should choose to call it the art of creating landscape' (Walpole quoted in Turner, 1987).

Landscape design is now perceived to be all of these things: functional, spatial and pictorial, each making demands at different levels of perception. Among the eighteenth century 'Improvers', Lancelot 'Capability' Brown was supreme – not so much for imitating nature but for transforming the English vernacular landscape. His interest was spatial rather than visual, expressed through movement along changing axes among serpentine forms. But space is indivisible. Now that the social balance has shifted, we are beginning to appreciate the importance of the relationship between space and place in the city as well as the country, and the relevance of character and atmosphere to both.

Plato had introduced the idea of geometry as the science of space, which was further defined by Aristotle in his theory of place (*topos*). Space was seen as the sum of all places, a dynamic field with directions and qualitative properties (Norberg-Schulz, 1971). This can be described in terms of landscape and settlement, explained as *space* and *character*. 'Whereas *space* denotes the three-dimensional organization of the elements which make up a place, *character* denotes the general atmosphere which is the most comprehensive property of any place' (Norberg-Schulz, 1980). The geometry of settlement derives primarily from the Platonic forms, which we are accustomed to see against the seemingly formless background of nature. But nature's forms are equally potent, although less explicitly expressed, except in the very large and the very small. In choosing native materials and serpentine forms for his green architecture, Brown came much nearer to a true appreciation of nature than his predecessors. Also, inevitably, he distanced himself from the garden-makers, who increasingly saw gardens more in terms of ornamental trees and decorative patterns of small plants.

As 'the landscape style' spread over Europe and much of the world, in England it seemed to merge with the agricultural vernacular, more functional than gardens were ever expected to be. In this it had something in common with the work of the engineers, who from the 1760s were transforming the countryside with systems of canals, roads and railways to serve the burgeoning industries. These, and the simple honest structures with which they were associated, emphasized the separation that had developed between designers of the 'aesthetic' and of the 'functional'. Also the revolutionary development of iron and steel permitted the expression of structural stresses much more precisely than had been possible with the stone of Gothic cathedrals: an expression of natural forces that can be seen – for example in the great suspension bridges – as the expression of a true union between art and nature.

The endless fascination of gardens as private microcosms of landscape has encouraged a separate evolution of the garden as an independent art form. Typically enclosed and relatively small, they may be amateur or professional, traditional or modern, good or bad: expressing particular ideas of time, space and form, sound and scent, texture and colour – or nothing in particular. In its private form the garden is an ideal place to experiment with ideas, materials and plants. Of its many public forms, the municipal practice of carpet-bedding has acquired the status of a folk-art, interestingly developed by Burle Marx in Brazil and Luz and his associates in Baden-Baden (see p.58). Also it has converged with civic design traditions of courtyards and public spaces, and with 'environmental art'; all important components of urban open space. In many of these, plants have no place, nature being represented by the use of water, the sky (including even passing clouds in

the case of Lucio Costa's centre for Brasilia) and the careful manipulation of light and colour.

While the value of such creative proving grounds for open space design is clear, as demonstrated in recent civic work in France and Spain (see p.76) by a variety of designers, there are dangers. Firstly there is the tendency towards abstraction – of the development of an ephemeral art that is limited in its appeal, to the eye and the camera. (There is a parallel in Picasso's fear that abstraction might give us, instead of pure painting, merely pure paint.) Secondly, there is already a 'designer culture' that is self-regarding, celebrated in books and journals, but divorced from natural realities: in particular, from the sense of unity between man and nature in which time and place are fundamental considerations. The expression of abstract and literary ideas may present interesting challenges with exciting effects, but they can easily slide into the irrelevance of clip-on architecture, as described in some studio jargon. 'We should reference hi-tech at the main entrance, so that becomes the vernacular' (Silver, 1980).

Landscape architecture has not yet fallen victim to such extravagant language, but the reason has more to do with a conservative suspicion of *avant-garde* 'design' than with any coherent alternative. The language of landscape is still the language of space, developed in common with architecture during the Renaissance. We speak of views and vistas, axes and desire lines, prospect and refuge, terms recently complemented by the spatial language used to describe the experience of serial vision (Cullen, 1971). Cullen regretted that the true meaning of 'townscape' has been overshadowed by a preoccupation with 'vernacular' details. Similarly, much of the great creative potential of landscape design has been dissipated by a preoccupation with the private, the decorative and the ephemeral.

Design, which may be seen as 'the conscious and intuitive effort to impose meaningful order' (Papanek, 1985), embraces all levels of creative input and perception, from the basic material to the finished product. As in the creations of nature, it must *work*. In land and building this is summed up in the idea of the vernacular: that which arises from human needs and available resources, in response to natural and human conditions – aptly described as 'environmental wisdom' (Turan, 1990). These basic qualities cannot be ignored or dispensed with, any more than they can be added. The environmental knowledge, if not wisdom, that is available to us now is infinitely greater than it has ever been. As well as displaying the hi-tech of industry, we need to use the much more sophisticated high technology of nature – planting trees to make fresh air and change the climate, and plants to clean water and soil – and we must learn again to cherish land, not just for nature, but for ourselves.

Our physical retreat from nature has been marked by many different interpretations – religious, philosophical, social, ecological, scientific – and expressed pictorially, spatially, functionally. No one alone has been satisfactory, each being the product of reductionist thinking. But they are, in many ways, complementary. Looking down from the air at the growth patterns of our civilization, we can see both order and chaos. The order appears generally in two ways: the 'organic' order that we call the vernacular, and the superimposed geometric order which derives largely from the cultures of Greece and Rome. Each is the product of planning and design. Chaos occurs at the edges and when the process is too random or too fast.

Whichever way we face the next millenium – either by continuing profligate commercial growth, or by consolidating our phenomenal assets in a renewed partnership with nature – it is only by *design* that we can create and sustain an environment worthy of our children.

CHAPTER 1

Connections

Only connect (E. M. Forster, *Howard's End*)

1.1 Cultures

> Art and science are uniquely human actions, outside
> the range of anything that an animal can do. And here
> we see that they derive from the same human faculty:
> the ability to visualize the future, to foresee what may
> happen and plan to anticipate it, and to represent it to
> ourselves in images ...
>
> (Jacob Bronowski, *The Ascent of Man*)

As binary beings we are drawn to opposites. We seek
symmetry and balance, finding harmony in contrasts: in
horizontal and vertical forms, in rough and smooth
textures, in complementary colours and in the achromatic black and white. Some of these are archetypal,
carrying meanings which go back to the beginnings of
culture. Darkness and light, left- and right-handedness,
even male and female/man and woman, have become
associated with such prototype symbols as good and
bad – the permitted and the forbidden (Leach, 1970).
The peculiar bureaucracy of our lives – the need for
order – allows our language to run away with us,
distorting ideas to fit the imagined patterns of
opposites. Order and chaos, art and science, science and
theology, idealism and materialism, the objective and
the subjective, the verbal and the visual, culture and
nature.

Architecture and landscape design fit uneasily into this
pattern of dualisms – at one level complementary, at
another opposed. Also they have themselves been
divided by fashionable arguments about the formal and
the informal, between the Classical and the Gothic or
traditional, the traditional and the modern, between
architecture as an art distinct from the science of
engineering – and both distinct from the vernacular.

Arts and sciences

Recognition of the growing division between the arts
and the sciences led C.P. Snow to express his concern in
The Two Cultures (1959) based on his experience as a
scientist at Cambridge University and as a writer.

> I believe the intellectual life of the whole of western society is
> increasingly being split into two polar groups. . . . At one pole
> we have the literary intellectuals – at the other scientists, and
> as the most representative, the physical scientists. Between the
> two a gulf of mutual incomprehension . . . sometimes hostility
> and dislike. . . . They have a curious distorted image of each
> other. (Snow, 1959).

Although Snow was working in England, his experience
of interviewing and contact with many thousands of
graduate scientists and engineers led him to conclude
that the problem was much more far-reaching, although
variable in degree. In England the situation has been
exacerbated, firstly by a strong and lasting belief in the
advantages of specialization, and secondly by the
tendency to allow social reforms to become crystallized.

The effect is that considerable numbers of the population reach the age of eighteen with an advanced understanding of a few subjects but are only half-educated in
the remainder. The problem has long been recognized
by educationalists, but only seems to exercise governments when there is a perceived shortage of candidates
for particular disciplines, perhaps arising from the want
of inspired teaching and certainly attributable to the
difficulty of learning scientific 'language'.

From his position among the scientific élite, Snow saw
the sciences as much more of a cultural entity than the
arts, both in an intellectual and in an anthropological

sense. Whether they were 'pure' or applied, physical or biological, he found common attitudes, common standards, assumptions and modes of reasoning. Even when they did not fully understand each other's discipline – and he admitted that pure scientists had limitations with regard to some applied sciences and engineering – they were able to communicate in ways which cut across barriers of religion, politics and class (Snow, 1959). The reason is not that scientists are essentially different from anyone else; the attitudes are inculcated by scientific training – the application of an intellectual rigour with demands that nothing can be accepted unless proven. The principle of 'objective reality' had become the bedrock of the sciences as they began to emerge from the theological cultures of the Middle Ages.

The dependence of the arts on a wide range of mental processes acknowledging the importance of feeling and emotion, tends to place them outside the scientific pale. They are commonly believed to be less demanding of intellectual rigour: a soft option too easily associated with 'the fuzzy fringe', liberalism, leftism and, often, ecology, although the language is different from that of Snow's intellectual élite. The intransigence of his pure scientists was only matched by that of his 'literary intellectuals' whose élitism can be seen to date back almost to the foundation of Oxford and Cambridge Universities. Even the title 'intellectual' had been monopolized by the literary *cognoscenti* of Cambridge in the 1930s. The literary and artistic culture carries undertones of taste and class that hark back to eighteenth-century England, and beyond to the Renaissance courts of France and Italy, where the cultural division began to take place. That the division was in large part social, is indicated by the experience of Leonardo da Vinci.

Leonardo da Vinci (1452–1519), whom we are inclined to regard as the model *uomo úniversale* (Universal man) of the Italian Renaissance, complained bitterly of his exclusion from the Humanist intellectual circles of Florence because he had not attended university and had no Latin and little Greek.

Because I am not a literary man some pretentious person will think that they may reasonably blame me by alleging that I am an unlettered man . . . they will say that because I have no letters I cannot express well what I want to treat of. . . . And if they despise me, an inventor, how much more could they – who are not inventors but trumpeters and declaimers of the works of others – be blamed (Leonardo da Vinci in Gimpel, 1988).

Rather than gaining recognition for the brilliance of his achievements both in the 'arts' and the 'sciences', he seems to have been regarded – at least by some of his contemporaries – as little more than a technician and manual worker (Gimpel 1988). Leonardo's experience

hints at the growing division between master and craftsman – the one who thinks (or designs) – and the one who works with his hands: an imbalance that is only now beginning to be corrected.

The sense of balance

Balance in our perceptions should match the symmetry of our bodies, which is reflected in our desire for balance in the environment. Because of the large amount of information with which our senses are confronted, certain perceptual economies are necessary. These are facilitated by the two lobes of the brain, each of which controls the motor functions of the opposite side of the body. Each also has control over different sensory functions. The left hemisphere controls spoken and written language, numerical and scientific skills, and reasoning; the right determines musical and artistic awareness, space and pattern perception, insight, imagination, and the generation of mental images of sight, sound, touch, taste and smell. As information is readily passed between the two hemispheres, the lateralization of function can only rarely be detected (Tortora and Anagnostakos, 1984).

Another, more obscure dichotomy seems to occur in the perception of colour, between the right hemisphere of the brain and the limbic system of the cerebral cortex, as reported by Dr Peter Smith. While the former appears to have 'the monopoly . . . [of being] responsive to the more subtle colours which are described as "cerebral" or "sophisticated" . . . outside the limited range of the primary and exotic', the limbic system is responsive to those colours of 'high chroma, brightness, shine and glitter' for their impact and exotic quality, to which symbolic meanings with archetypal origins are ascribed. While we are at pains to seek 'tasteful' solutions with one part of our brains, equating emotion with vulgarity; 'for limbic satisfaction it is necessary to go to market places, Picadilly Circus or Las Vegas' (Smith, 1976). Smith notes the critical tension between the elements causing a cerebral response and those stimulating emotion, either through the content or the medium. Rembrandt, Turner and Rouault achieved this bi-polar tension through both: Mondrian strikes a critical balance 'predominantly through colour stripped of cognitive meaning' (ibid).

This dualism of perception can go some way towards explaining the apparent contradiction between the ideal of form in Classical Greek temple sculptures, and the 'vulgarity' of the way in which they were painted. 'Statuary was deeply dyed with garish pigments. The marble figure of a woman found on the Athenian Acropolis was tinctured red, green, blue and yellow. Quite often statues had red lips, glowing eyes made of precious stones and even artificial eyelashes' (Porter, 1982). Another, anonymous writer reported a freshly unearthed pediment with sculptured 'flesh, reddish in tone; globes of eyes yellow, iris green, with a hole in the centre filled with black; black outlines to eyebrows and eyelids; hair and beard bright blue . . . circle of brown around the nipples' (ibid).

Science and theology

The cultural debate has recently re-erupted in newspaper correspondence between scientists and theologians, the former using the weapon of practicality against the spirituality of the latter. It is certainly true that without the application of scientific methods, civilization would not have advanced, or even occurred. Nor could it have advanced by means of these alone – a fact which is often overlooked. Also, it is important to remember that a great deal of science derives from speculation, which, like bad art, is better forgotten. The advantages and disadvantages of both science and theology should be measured in their value to society. There are moral, if not spiritual dimensions to every question, from dealing with the 100,000 year legacy of the nuclear industry, to the excavation of channels for fibre-optic communications – both of which have an important impact on the environment. Also, we might perhaps pause to wonder what will be communicated in 500 channels. The threat of science as commonly perceived is that of the unknown and the unintelligible, which is often equated with modernism. Pollution is now no longer something that can be clearly seen in water or in the air, it lurks insidiously in every part of the environment, and scientists are blamed: 'Like some expansionist power, science has swollen its claims and its frontiers until the petty kingdom of the self has lost all will to resist' (George Walden MP, former Science Minister quoted by Joe Schwartz, reported in the *Daily Telegraph*, quoted in the *Guardian*, June 1992). But does he really mean science? Why not politicians who give licence to scientists to operate in society? He is surely referring to that which is now described as *scientism* – the doctrine that science and science alone can save humanity.

True science must be seen, like art, as the interpretation of life – of nature and natural forces in all their amazing complexity; the elegance of classical mechanics that enables us to understand matter in motion, the mathematical vibrations of a stretched string; the principles of gravity that make the apple fall, keep us upright and cause the sun and moon to control the tides. Or is it all the work of God? Either way we should beware the dangers of extremism.

Mechanism now lives next to fanaticism. Societies are in the hands either of the commercially powerful but spiritually empty or, to a lesser extent, in the hands of fanatical zealots under the sway of unscientific myths and emotion (Edelman, 1992).

Class, culture and taste

Extremism in any field is dangerous, and we have seen how political movements have manipulated people by every means at their disposal, including art and design and especially advertising. The sociologist Herbert Gans has identified five categories of 'taste-culture' which Charles Jencks has applied to society in Britain – a country in which ideas of class are never far beneath the surface. The first, *producers' high culture*, is represented by the avant-garde, the 'cutting edge', the modernists and post-modernists, the fashion taste-makers and cultural writers. A close second is the *traditional high culture*, represented by Royalty, the aristocracy, the country house and 'county' cultures, supported by the nostalgia industry with a strong source of energy in the *nouveau riches*, all aiming to uphold the traditional values of the nineteenth century, which they see as having been usurped by modernism. The *mid-cult* of the classless middle classes is a large and amorphous group frequently targeted by the culture industry, and novelists such as Jeffrey Archer, and musicians such as Leonard Bernstein. The fourth-category combines the lower middle classs and the upper working class, represented by Margaret Thatcher, Ronald Reagan, John Major, the Beatles, Madonna, David Lynch and many of the 'most vital and vulgar'. Finally, the bottom ten per cent exists in a *culture of poverty and dependency*, untargeted by any culture industry (Jencks, 1992). Jencks suggests a floating sixth category including the very young and the very old, feminists, ethnic minorities and immigrant intellectuals, who often reach the top of the British professions and contribute greatly to the whole culture. It is a game that can be played endlessly, varying the counters to give different combinations. But the effects on society of such cultural type-casting should not be underestimated: they are taken very seriously by the 'taste-makers' – those in the design and advertizing industries whose business is the manipulation of fashion.

The familiar modernist versus traditionalist battle is waged between the first two cultures, represented on the one hand by leading architects and designers, and on the other by establishment figures. The wish of the latter to return to 'traditional values' arises from their discomfiture in feeling that they can no longer control their environment, or even understand it. But the values of this second culture include a genuine and strongly-expressed concern for the natural environment, which has little place in those of the former. The strongly traditional basis for landscape design would place it in the second category, but with uncomfortable reservations about the hunting, shooting and fishing associations of the conservationist lobby and strong leanings – particularly among the young – towards the avant-garde. There is, however, a sense of pervasive nostalgia dragging landscape architecture and architecture alike, back towards an 'arts-and-crafts' inspired view of the modern world. While the design languages of the past offer the comfort of familiar images for the public and many practitioners, modernism – at least as it is understood – seems tainted by social failure and the avant-garde seems fraught with risk. Undoubtedly this is a reason for the popularity of Post-Modernism, that assemblage of styles that has yet to find a true identity.

Whether all of these fragmented cultures could or should ever achieve homogeneity is a matter for speculation, which raises questions about the criteria for judgement. Historically, the latter has been used often to suppress other peoples' tastes in supporting an insecure minority. Cultural integration, Jencks suggests – while admitting that it would 'be unpopular with some people, as well as far off – would depend upon a world culture and *a world religion that is consonant with science*' (author's italics), believing the latter prospect at least conceivable,

now that the new sciences have shifted from a mechanistic view to a more organic world view: the Gaia hypothesis, the 20 or so 'Chaos' sciences and non-linear dynamics are all pointing in this direction (Jencks, 1992).

Wisely he does not say how long we may have to wait.

1.2 Environment

The way human beings see themselves in relation to nature is fundamental to all cultures; thus the first fact of architecture is the natural world, the second is the relationship of human structures to the topography of the world, and the third is the relationship of all these structures to each other, comprising the human community as a whole.
(Vincent Scully, *Architecture: The Natural and the Man-made, in Denatured Visions*)

Environment is too grand a word – too cosmic in its implications – to describe effectively the familiar places in which we live. It now means everything from the ozone layer to the microbes in our drains. The environment *is* everything, everywhere. No longer can it be considered only in terms of the houses we build, the food we eat, the water we drink and the air we breathe. We now know that everything has a hidden cost in materials, transport, labour, the community and society; juggled incessantly by the market economies, thwarted by the social problems of burgeoning populations, but

chargeable, ultimately, to the environment. Inevitably, we are all participants in this process, aspiring to progress ourselves. While enjoying the present we must all be aware, however dimly, that the situation cannot last. Fearing the future – still suspicious of 'the modern' – many seek sanctuary in images of the past, either in genuine attempts to return to nature, or in notions of a Golden Age. The dilemma of the present – which has perhaps always been a dilemma – is the uncertainty of the future. 'Past and future attract – and repel in quite different ways' (Lowenthal, 1985).

Looking back at past cultures, we see them as complete, as though their course had been run. But the process is continuous as one culture merges into another. We in Europe are the living product of many layers of cultural development. The early societies progressed by virtue of improvements in technology, which were the foundations of urban settlements. The great European civilizations of Greece and Rome, Islam (although we tend to disregard it), Christendom and the Renaissance, were all built upon these foundations and have continued the civilizing process inexorably. As Europeans we are all part of this ancient and continuing cultural mix:

The past remains integral to us all, individually and collectively. We must concede the ancients their place, as I have argued. But their place is not simply back there, in a separate and foreign country; it is assimilated in ourselves, and resurrected into an ever-changing present (Lowenthal, 1985).

All the problems of our own society can be seen in microcosm in those of the past. The felling of forests, plundering of resources, pollution, waste, greed, exploitation, and warfare, have been the accompaniments of all phases of dynamic growth. Even the machine, which William Morris tended to think of as our own special folly, has a long and respectable history. The real problem is one of understanding; which is also one of time: of having time to understand and develop effective solutions before the next great wave of progress has overtaken us. Mass-production is an aspect of this problem: but it has its roots both in the advancement of civilization and, in what may be seen as one of the consequences, over-population – 'more people, more houses, more amenities, faster communications and unfamiliar building materials' (Cullen, 1971). The inestimable value of science, technology and machinery, is that they can be directed towards solving the problems, if only we could learn to apply them rationally.

Patterns of civilization

It was first in animals and children, but later also in adults, that I observed the immensely powerful *need for regularity* – the need which makes them seek for regularities
(Karl Popper, *Objective Knowledge*)

Order in nature is apparent only in the very large and the very small. While minute organisms surprise us by their symmetry, the overall impression is one of irregularity induced by natural forces. Only rarely are man-made patterns fully integrated, for example in contour ploughing or irrigation terraces. Normally there is a contrast, as though we have found it necessary to express a certain defiance with bold geometric forms which stand out against the natural background. The circle, the square, the rectangle and the avenue are all ancient forms that signify the presence of man. Their expression in the landscape is essentially one of contrast.

A parallel might be drawn between the two main harmonies of colour: that of analogy, in which the colours are closely related, and complementary harmony in which the colours are directly opposed. There is, however, a point at which the geometry begins to dominate. This can be seen similarly in the long straight Roman roads, the great 'shafts of space' devised by Renaissance designers, and in canals, railways and the early motorways. Their expression can be interpreted in different ways: direct, functional, authoritarian, unimaginative. The first two were undoubtedly expressions of power – that of Rome and that of the Renaissance rulers – the others more particularly of the functionalist attitudes of engineers of our own time. In the latter cases there is often a dramatic increase in scale, contrasting with the less strident, more organic geometry of medieval towns and villages, and of the countryside: of what we call the vernacular.

The vernacular and the functional tradition

There is a common misconception that the vernacular is a kind of pure or innocent design, unspoilt by the aesthetic ideas of architects. 'Vernacular architecture does not go through fashion cycles. It is nearly immutable, indeed unimprovable, since it serves its purpose to perfection' (Rudofsky, 1964). But what is it, and what is the purpose that it so perfectly serves? In its simplest, purist form, it can be seen as a part of nature and the landscape. The mud architecture of the Dogon tribe in West Africa has strong similarities in form to those cellular structures made by mud-wasps. The material and technique of building are akin to those of pottery, and as with pots their function is simple. The function is also relatively simple in those aggregations of rooms with flat roofs which make such perfect cubic compositions of old villages around the Mediterranean. They were achieved with local materials, abundant labour, and almost complete self-sufficiency, informed by traditional 'environmental wisdom' (Turan, 1990). The 'landscape' spaces between them are a product of that same 'wisdom' applied to functional needs of

circulation, manoeuvring donkeys, selling goods and general living within the limitations imposed by land ownership, neighbours, and the qualities of the site itself. It is the combination of all these qualities, and the sense that each is the product of individual hands or decisions, made over a long period, that is so heart-warming. In this limited sense the vernacular deserves to be called organic, fitting the neat distinction made by the poet Coleridge in a lecture on Shakespeare in 1818: 'Form is mechanic when on any given material we impress a predetermined form, not necessarily arising out of the properties of the material.' Organic form, on the other hand, is innate: shaping itself from within, as it develops, so that 'the fullness of its development is one and the same with the perfection of its outward form' (Simonds, 1961).

There are several clear reasons why the vernacular of this definition can no longer be considered relevant – except perhaps in examples of individual dwellings. The first is time; the others are connected with materials, energy, labour, services and the innumerable requirements of modern living. But the idea of the vernacular is elusive for other reasons. Much of it is what we might equally associate with engineering, for example the stone circles and avenues of the Bronze Age, the timber cantilever and the rope suspension bridges of the Himalayas, and water-wheels and dams described by Rudofsky. Many of them belong equally to the industrial 'functional tradition' described by Richards and De Maré (1958). These include buildings and designs of many periods, from windmills to textile mills, that have been associated with industry – primarily with the industrial growth of the last two centuries. Canals, and canal architecture, which feature prominently, are significant because they have developed their own folklore, also they are, above all, elements of landscape design. Probe a little deeper, and we find that this 'industrial vernacular', dating from the 1770s when the canal building boom started – to provide transport for the growing industries – depended, like the railways that followed, not upon local styles based upon local materials, but upon corporate styles often using transported materials. There is also an urban equivalent – which we might call *urban vernacular* – of buildings, walls, street furniture, paving, which belongs to, and was made possible by the development of industry (see p.12).

While the vernacular of traditional agriculture tends to have a more organic quality, there is no clear dividing line between it and the use of mechanistic geometry that is more typical of industry. Usually, the two approaches are mixed – such is our need for order and regularity. Occasionally the imposed structure effects a transformation, as, for example, in the spatial planning of the Renaissance. There is a clear logic to both approaches, although the objectives may differ. Also, it should be noted that logic does not always apply in design, any more than it does in the vernacular. In art it applies still less: 'The artist prefers the submissiveness of amorphous matter' (Arnheim, 1968).

Experiencing the environment

The emphasis on vision in our assessment of the two architectures – that of building and that of the landscape – inhibits our appreciation of more profound qualities. Since the landscape can no longer be viewed as merely a pictorial setting for the building, having revealed itself as a living entity that affects all aspects of our lives, a more penetrating analysis is called for. Appleton (1986) wisely chooses the word experience to describe his explorations into the nature of landscape and our responses to it. Actors and dancers have been described as 'hybrids of art and nature' for the ways in which they explore space with their bodies (Arnheim, 1974). This applies also to sports, for which the 'stage' is of landscape dimensions. The analogy gives added meaning to the courtly gardens of the Renaissance which had distinct theatrical functions in dance and drama, and there are affinities with stage-sets in the design method used by Humphry Repton in the Red Books.

The landscape gardens of Capability Brown were 'fundamentally physical and intellectual in their appeal', according to Christopher Hussey (Stroud, 1975). They were, it is true, inspired by the gentle atmosphere of nature portrayed in Richard Wilson's paintings, but Brown regarded his method on the ground as more akin to literary compositions: 'setting a comma here, a full-stop there' in a letter from Brown to Hannah More, as he manipulated the horizontal and vertical serpentine curves dictated by the ideas of Beauty expressed by Hogarth and Burke. Burke describes the effect, not just in pictorial terms, but in terms of movement:

Most people have observed the sort of sense they have had of being swiftly drawn in an easy coach on a smooth turf, with gradual ascents and declivities. This will give a better idea of the Beautiful than almost anything else (Burke, *Ideas of the Sublime and the Beautiful*, 1757).

The passage recalls the sense of rhythm which we readily associate with horse-riding. It relates to our sense of balance as investigated in the 'ecological optics' of J. J. Gibson (1979). 'Walking or riding towards an object on ground level and fixing our eyes on it, we see it not only increase in size but we also perceive "a panoramic flow" of the surround which opens up before us and swings round in a regular pattern. In this situation the asymmetry of the flow will either denote that we have swayed from our course and must adjust it, or that the ground is not level' (Gombrich, 1984).

This is a means of monitoring our own balance and movement which is also achieved by our assumptions that still water is level and that the light normally comes from above (ibid).

The interest in movement and speed is irresistable; and it is, essentially, an outdoor – landscape – activity. There is a hint of it in the painting by Turner *Rain, Steam and Speed* (1844), celebrating the first great wave of industrial progress, which transformed both the landscape and the *view* of it. This view – from a moving vehicle – has become the focus of consideration in *A View from the Road* by Appleyard, Lynch and Myer (1964), in which they compare the 'personal mastery of space' on skis or on a motor-cycle, with that of a car. The relative delicacy and ease of control of the former 'vehicles' reinforce the sense of outside contact with the environment. In the latter case, the enclosed vehicle emphasizes the difference in scale between the observer and the vastness of (landscape) space – from which it provides a refuge.

The travelling eye

The formal gardens of le Notre had developed on the principle of fixed point perspective, in which the levels and the proportions of the elements were carefully controlled to present a series of contrived views to the approaching visitor (Hazlehurst, 1980). In Brown's landscapes this was not possible. Although there were still vistas, the curving roads and the informal planting meant that they were constantly changing in a manner expressed by the Chinese convention of 'the travelling eye'. Chinese painting was a method of representing three dimensions in one plane with many viewpoints, a process involving the spectator in both time and space, which reached the height of its expression in scroll painting. In the garden this shifting perspective is described as 'the hovering view region' or 'seeing the small from the viewpoint of the large' (Shen Kua, eleventh century) and as being appropriate for the simulation of nature. There is a parallel in the work of Cezanne, who painted variations of the same scene from slightly differing viewpoints: a principle developed by the Cubists, and later by David Hockney (Johnston, 1991).

The architectural application of this principle described by Gordon Cullen (1971) as 'serial vision' is a means of portraying the changing experiences as the eye moves along an irregular axis or series of axes. In this way it is possible to record and analyse both the *existing view* and the *emerging view*. It is based upon the *art of relationship*: the now rather obvious principle that nothing is ever seen in isolation. The environment comprises: 'buildings, trees, nature, water, traffic, advertisements . . . . for a city is a dramatic event in the environment'. Words such as progression, rhythm, punctuation, enclosure, intimacy, entanglement and surprise, are part of the language used to describe places with individual qualities of 'colour, texture, scale, style, character, personality, uniqueness' (Cullen, 1971). Although the method offered new insights into the nature of places, it has had the unfortunate effect of superficial interpretation as a civic style of decoration with cobbles and bollards. For this, perhaps, the name 'townscape' must take a share of the blame. Like landscape, it is frequently seen as a cosmetic veneer. But the future has no limits. The method suggests all kinds of applications – including the vital dimension of colour, which the original medium of reproduction precluded – for urban and rural environments of all types: perhaps also employing the computer techniques of 'virtual reality' – provided that we appreciate their limitations, for we must make the judgements.

The question of evaluation

In art and architecture the use of the word *aesthetic* implies accepted standards of education or taste; in the landscape, no such criteria can be assumed to apply. Therein lies a difficulty of the subject, and a reason for its uneasy links with architecture. Cullen's approach depends less on value judgements, than on relative and transient effects. In this sense it has a close affinity with the Prospect-Refuge theory. Cullen speaks of an enclave open to the exterior:

'an eddy in which footsteps echo and the light is lessened in intensity. Set apart from the hurly-burly of traffic, it has the advantage of commanding the scene from a position of safety and strength.'

(Cullen, *Townscape*, 1971).

From experience of the dangers of our own surroundings, we understand well the need for enclosed 'safe' places which seem to offer protection and provide vantage points; a principle that can be applied equally to town and country. This concept is the basis of the Prospect-Refuge Theory developed by Jay Appleton in his explorations into 'The Experience of Landscape' (1986). He suggests a link with the habitat theories derived from the study of animal and bird behaviour:

'Habitat theory postulates that aesthetic pleasure in landscape derives from the observer experiencing an environment favourable to the satisfaction of his biological needs. Prospect-refuge theory postulates that, because of the ability to see without being seen is an intermediate step in the satisfaction of many of those needs, the capacity of an environment to ensure the achievement of *this* becomes a more immediate source of aesthetic satisfaction.'

(Appleton, *The Experience of Landscape*, 1986)

Clearly the word aesthetic has no relevance to the world of animals; but it must also be called into question in terms of our own cultural values. The idea of a tangible quality of beauty which Brown attempted to embody in his 'natural' landscapes, was changed irrevocably by the cultural fragmentation which followed in the 19th century (Dixon-Hunt, 1993). Now that modernism has effectively broken the links which united nature, beauty and art, we should be wiser if we limited ourselves to the consideration of experience.

1.3 Nature

Nature is the only book that teems with meaning on every page.
(Goethe)

Nature without learning is like a blind man; learning without Nature, like a maimed one; practice without both, incomplete.
(Plutarch)

Conflict is endemic to nature. All species struggle to survive, both within the group and within the environment. But there is a further, internal conflict in human beings caused by the paradox of being at once a part of and outside, nature. This is reflected in various ways in different religions. Hindus and Buddhists both recognize *dharma*, 'the essential quality which unites all beings, human, animal and plant, with the universe and ultimately with the source of their existence' (Prime, 1992)' Jews, Christians and Muslims are united in a belief in their own primacy in the world, bestowed by an external God – a creed that has become a fundamental tenet of modernism. The Old Testament makes much of the land, but as a possession, and while both the Bible and the Koran give good 'green' advice, there is no question about man's supremacy.

Buddhism teaches that there is no independent self. When it spread to China it was subjected to the teachings of Lao-Tzu (*c*.604–517 BC) expressed in the *Tao-te-Ching*. The *Tao* is the principle which governs nature, and, at the same time, the reality from which the world emerged. *Tao* originates things effortlessly and spontaneously: it 'acts by not acting' a principle expressed in the blank spaces of Chinese painting (Rawson and Legeza, 1973). In the consideration of time and space, activity and inactivity, *Tao* gets much nearer than the other creeds to the complexities and apparent contradictions that are at the heart of nature. 'Nothing which happens . . . ever repeats itself exactly'. On the other hand the 'uncarved block', 'mother', 'matrix of time', including both 'being and not being', incorporating 'the Great Whole of continuous duration, infinite space and infinite change', does not itself change (Rawson and Legeza, 1973). Although it is not difficult to see how such esoteric ideas can be lost upon the burgeoning millions now clamouring for capitalism, Buddhism has had a profound effect upon ecology, which must be regarded as a faith, if not a religion. 'Buddhist economics' are at the heart of the principles set out by Fritz Schumacher, author of *Small is Beautiful* (1973), advocating a 'middle way' based upon maximum well-being and minimum consumption (Schwartz, 1992).

People

As early as 1798 Malthus had predicted disaster for mankind. Since populations tend to grow more or less geometrically, doubling every twenty-five years, and food production grows only arithmetically, our inevitable fate towards the end of the nineteenth century would be starvation, deprivation, mass deaths through famine and disease, and a general collapse of civilization. He has been discredited by those who accuse environmentalists of a kind of *Schadenfreude* in predicting 'doom and gloom'. But Paul Kennedy, in *Preparing for the Twenty-first Century* (1993), argues that Malthus was absolutely correct in his population predictions; except that he did not foresee the power of science and technology to increase agricultural and industrial production. While the population of Britain increased four-fold in the nineteenth century, production actually increased fourteen-fold.

Such increases, even if they were sustainable, do not alone solve the world problem of starvation, as we are experiencing today in the case of Africa. Even when the problems of storage and distribution are solved, there are further problems of social instability caused by the migrations of populations, pollution, deforestation and the loss of cultivable land. We still see these problems from afar, but there are clear indications that they are coming nearer. The effects of global warming alone – of which the threat advances and recedes according to differing scientific views and commercial interests – could be flooding of low-lying areas of land which would increase the numbers of refugees in the world by tens of millions. Even without such a catastrophe, we have dramatically increasing numbers of refugees likely to add to our overcrowded cities, in which poverty and unemployment are already increasing urban decay. Whatever the charitable reaction, it is clear that none of our political systems is yet equipped to deal with such emergencies. Politics – 'the art of the possible' – is still associated with short-term solutions, and nature is nothing, if not long term. There is, however, hope in an alliance between nature and economics – that subject which does seem to excite all governments.

A link between the two was established by the naturalist, Frank Fraser-Darling, in the BBC Reith Lectures (1970) under the title 'Wilderness and Plenty', based on the effects of population, pollution and the generosity of the earth. Five hundred years ago, religion and philosophy were shaken by the discovery that the earth was spherical and finite. But the population was small. Now that the population has increased phenomenally (from some 1000 million at the time Malthus was writing to 5¼ billion today), the shock waves are beginning to be seen as biological. As a biologist, Darling was able to bring the subject down to earth, focusing on basic human needs in the context of a rapidly growing industrial world economy. His voice gave authority to the growing environmental movement, and it reminds us still that the environment begins at home.

There can be no greater moral obligation in the environmental field than to ease out the living space and replace dereliction by beauty. Most people will never know wilderness although its existence will not be a matter of indifference to them. The near landscape is valuable and lovable because of its nearness, not something to be disregarded and shrugged off; it is where children are reared and what they take away in their minds to their long future. What ground could be more hallowed?

(Fraser-Darling, 1970).

Ecology

Ecology was the science which could interpret the fragments of evidence that told us something was wrong with the world – dead birds, oil in the sea, poisoned crops, the population explosion. . . . What it meant was – everything links up. . . . Here was a new morality, and a strategy for survival rolled into one.'
(Anne Chisholm, *Philosophers of the Earth*)

The common scientific view of ecology is one of 'the interaction of organisms and energy flows in a closed system' (Bramwell, 1989). But ecological ideas have become associated with widely diverse situations. They might, for example, be concerned with the conservation of specific energy flows on a site as small as a one-acre wetland site, or alternatively, with the weather pattern resulting from the Amazon rainforest. The word is derived from *oekologie*, which has its roots in the Greek word for house, *oikos*. Originally it was used as co-terminus with ethology, the study of animal behaviour in its environment, and with *oekonomie*, the concept of 'economical' household management, implying activities which have moral significance for the survival of the group (ibid).

The ecology movement, or movements – for it is an imprecise term – originated in the holistic and anti-mechanistic approach to biology promoted by the German zoologist Ernst Haeckel in the late nineteenth century, and the relatively recent development of economics, known as energy economics, focused on the problem of scarce and non-renewable resources. When the two came together in the 1970s, the first, which had lost credibility because of its links with Nazi Germany, was boosted by the firmer scientific basis of the latter. Ecological theories have developed most significantly in the industrialized countries: Britain, Germany and North America, with some contributions from French and Russian scientists. In Europe, Germany and Britain are most noted for their mobilized environmental groups, and for their small, but growing political influence through the Green movement (Bramwell, 1989).

As the errors and disasters have become more obvious, the movement has grown, attracting many serious practitioners and a few politicians, as well as the inevitable fringe groups; and it has generated a wealth of published material. Edward Goldsmith, founder and editor of *The Ecologist* has expressed the principles of the movement in sixty-six articles of faith (Goldsmith, 1992). According to Goldsmith, ecology is holistic, combining matter and spirit; teleological in its acceptance of evolution as purposeful (for the earth), and qualitative rather than quantitative. Goldsmith attacks both academics and society in general for their espousal of *modernism*:

One of the two most fundamental tenets of the world view of modernism and its academic paradigms is that all benefits, and therefore our welfare and our real wealth, are derived from the man-made world; this means, in effect, that they are the product of science, technology and industry, and of the economic development that these make possible. The inestimable benefits provided by the normal functioning of the Biosphere – such as a favourable and stable climate, fertile soil and fresh water, without which life on this planet is not possible – are totally ignored and assigned no value of any kind.
    The second fundamental tenet of the world view of modernism . . . is that to maximize all benefits, and hence our welfare and our wealth, we must maximize and venerate economic development (Goldsmith, 1992).

Although the attack may be seen as an attack upon science and scientists, it is really directed against the remarkably blinkered view of the world expressed through *scientism* – the elevation of scientific procedures into a dominant world view claiming to address and provide solutions to all major human problems.

Ecology is still seen as a 'soft' science, and such protests – even from highly responsible sources, provoke counter-attacks. Armageddon has, after all, been predicted on many occasions since biblical times, usually in relation to significant points in the calendar. A recent writer even uses biblical language: 'We have built a greenhouse, a human creation, where once there bloomed a sweet and wild garden' (McKibbern, 1989).

A counter-attack is led by Richard North (1990), who describes 'environmentalists' as misanthropes who dislike this process of populating the world. His argument is supported by impressive statistics on the achievements of science in reducing child death-rates, increased longevity, and increased food production in some of the poorest countries. 'Better management', he writes, 'will restore environments to productive vigour'. But he admits that 'that the world cannot sustain expanding populations indefinitely . . . the greenhouse effect may damage the livelihoods of millions of people. The laboratories of the world may unleash some dreadful mutants. We may make the world much uglier than it is now. . . . On the other hand, this brilliant species may thrive and continue in its hugely successful, and evolving, relationship with nature' (North, 1990).

In spite of the political tone, seeming to advocate the survival only of the fittest, there are hints of doubt. In what ways do we enjoy a 'hugely successful, and evolving, relationship with nature'? And can we really afford to make the world *uglier*?

The question can be answered in two ways: in terms of our own individual living environments and that of the planet Earth. We have a responsibility for both, but the first is inevitably the subject of our greater attention, because it is the new 'designed' landscape of the late twentieth century which is our habitat. Some of the ways in which we are dealing with both of these are disastrous for ourselves and perhaps herald the approaching end of our civilization. As for the planet, the future is written in the stars.

Gaia

Viewed from the distance of the moon, the astonishing thing about the earth . . . is that it is alive. The photographs show the dry pounded surface of the moon in the foreground, dead as an old bone. Aloft, floating free beneath the moist, gleaming membrane of bright blue sky, is the rising earth, the only exhuberant thing in this part of the cosmos.
                        (Lewis Thomas, *The Lives of a Cell*)

The idea that the Earth itself is alive had its origins in the search for life on Mars. James Lovelock, a scientist with a background in biology and medicine, managed to escape the narrow specialization and laboratory life that is the fate of many scientists, by joining NASA as an experimenter on its first lunar mission. This enabled him to consider the earth from a unique vantage point. The result, after several years of research and speculation, was the Gaia theory, named after the Greek Goddess of the Earth. The theory was baptized on the advice of William Golding, the novelist, who felt that anything alive deserved a name (Lovelock, 1988).

Gaia, the earth, has its own serene ecological balance, its own will to live. It is capable of preserving its own existence. It can shrug off disturbing intrusions, whether from comets or from man. Like any other species, Gaia has its own natural term. It lives and it will die. (From Anna Bramwell, *Ecology in the Twentieth Century*, on Gaia, 1990.)

In considering the three most powerful approaches to the study of the earth (first molecular biology – the understanding of those information-processing chemicals that are the genetic basis of all life on Earth; second physiology – the science concerned with living systems seen holistically; and third thermodynamics), Lovelock favours the last. This is the branch of physics that deals with time and energy, which connects living processes to the fundamental laws of the universe. Hitherto, the subject had made little progress beyond the quest of engineers to make steam engines more efficient. The first law of thermodynamics is about energy: that energy is always conserved. Some of the energy of sunlight falling upon leaves is reflected so that we see the leaves are green, some is absorbed and warms them, and some is transformed into food and oxygen. We eat the food, breathe the oxygen and use the sun's energy to move, to think and to keep warm.

The second law is about the dissymmetry of nature. When heat is converted to work, some of it is wasted. The redistribution of energy in the universe has direction: it is always running down. Hot objects cool; but cool objects never spontaneously become hot. Natural processes always move towards an increase of disorder, measured by entropy (Lovelock, 1988). By contrast, it is in the nature of man to strive for order.

The Gaia theory emphasizes most the significance of the individual organism. It is always from the action of individuals that powerful local, regional and global systems evolve. When the activity of the organism favours the environment as well as the organism itself, then its spread will be assisted. Eventually, the organism and the environmental changes associated with it will become global in extent. The reverse is also true, and any species that adversely affects the environment is doomed. But life goes on. So long as we continue to change the global environment against the natural order, we encourage our replacement with a more environmentally seemly species. Death and decay are certain, but they seem a small price to pay for the possession, even briefly, of life on this earth as an individual (Lovelock, 1988).

Of the many threats to the environment, Lovelock cites cars, cattle and chain-saws among the most pernicious. All are extremely useful, and relatively harmless on a small scale. On the global scale on which we use them they threaten our survival as a species. Nature has shown herself to be immensely resourceful, but she has no concern for humankind. She will survive until her own purpose is fulfilled.

1.4 Nature, art and design

What we have to find, therefore, is some touchstone outside the individual peculiarities of human beings, and the only touchstone which exists is *nature*. And by nature we mean the whole organic process of life and movement which goes on in the universe, a process which includes man, but which is indifferent to his genetic idiosyncrasies, his subjective reactions, and temperamental variations.

(Herbert Read *Education Through Art*)

When we walk by the edge of the sea we are bombarded by sensations. Our eyes feast upon the specks of light and colour reflected from the waves back towards the sand, the green shore and the far blue mountains. We feel the wind on our bodies, we taste and smell the salt sea air, and we are deafened by the sound of the waves as we watch them breaking into turbulent patterns of spirals, each one similar but never the same. We are conscious of the rhythm of the waves, their ebb and flow, responding like a pulse to the cosmic forces that control all life.

The spiral patterns associated with turbulence are the elemental patterns of creation and dissolution, similar to those which appear, at a vastly increased scale, in the storm clouds seen from weather satellites and in spiral nebulae. They appear when water flows over a weir, and, at a minute scale, when we stir cream into our coffee. They are spontaneous movements, like the unseen spiral patterns of sound made by whistling sea-birds. More tangible are the spiral growth patterns of mollusc shells, each designed to accommodate stages of regular growth for the life-span of their inhabitants – 'concrete' architectural versions of the spiral growth patterns of plants and trees. Contained within everything, we can now see the miraculous spiral patterns of DNA, the fundamental pattern of life.

Our experience – at once sensory, emotional, poetic and intellectual – draws upon all our senses, impinging equally on those areas of specialization which we choose to call 'arts' and 'sciences'. The 'beauty' can be found in any one of many different aspects, not merely in appearance. Nor can it be absolute. It resides more in some combination of the Greek mathematical conception of perfect form and our scientific understanding of function – the way things work, which is so elegantly expressed in the patterns of nature.

When we see how the branching of trees resembles the branching of arteries and the branching of rivers, how crystal grains look like soap bubbles and the plates of a tortoise shell, how the fiddle-heads of ferns, stellar galaxies and water emptying from the bath-tub spiral in a similar manner, then we cannot help wondering why nature uses only a few kindred forms in so many different contexts (Stevens, 1976).

Patterns of nature

The *spiral*, with the *wave* or *meander* and the patterns of *explosion* and *branching*, together represent the four basic patterns of organic growth, all of which we have adapted for our purposes. Each is a means of linking elements and occupying space, transmitting stresses and permitting growth. Each has its own characteristics.

Spirals and explosions represent two extremes. The spiral is compact, but circuitous, following a route in which time is not important. It is ideal for plant growth, and for staircases where space is limited. The explosion is direct both in time and distance from the centre to the outlying parts, but the sum total of the distance is enormous. Branching patterns are a compromise between the two. For transporting nutrients from the roots to the outermost leaves of the tree, they are ideal. For this the spiral is too circuitous and the explosion too extravagant: a tree cannot afford to sustain each of its leaves on a separate branch. The form of the flower-head, on the other hand, is usually determined by the need for a direct relationship between the centre and the perimeter. In practical terms the strength-weight ratio of the distance to the cross-sectional area of the ducts carrying nutrients from the centre to the extremities, is crucial, and in some cases, branching becomes necessary.

Branching is the commonest structure for all plants. But it occurs also, in common with the meander pattern, in rivers, in lightning and in the arterial systems of bodies. The meander is close to the spiral. Whereas a spiral is produced by one surface growing longer than the other, causing the form to curve round upon itself, a meander is produced by the growth of the surfaces varying in a periodic manner. The periodic tightening and relaxing of the muscles of a snake are the cause of its meandering movements, as are the muscles of our backbones. Slow rivers and slack seas use the meander, albeit in different ways, the former being much less regular and rhythmical. The form occurs compact in the human brain, in brain coral, and, microscopically, in garnet. We can identify it also in the seemingly tortured cross-sections of tulips and cabbages, and gnarled sections of wood and stone, but these are influenced by more complicated patterns of flow and stress, similar to those patterns of turbulence that express the polarities of order and chaos.

Form, stress and structure

> If the world were totally regular and homogenous, there would be no forces and no forms. Everything would be amorphous. But an irregular world tries to compensate for its own irregularities by fitting itself to them, and thereby takes on form.
> (Christopher Alexander, *Notes on the Synthesis of Form*.)

When we see how beams bend, how balloons and bubbles burst, we know that there is an optimum size for the material with which they are formed. We also know that small things are light and large things are heavy; a fly is so light that it can land on the ceiling; a beached whale so heavy that its weight can cause it to suffocate. The satisfaction afforded by the sight of large tent structures and suspension bridges – in which the forces of nature are so elegantly expressed – must be connected with the sense of this innate unity. It has a close parallel in our experience of the use of tools and other artefacts of which the form and function have evolved over the centuries to be appropriate extentions of the human and animal body – in the handle of a scythe, the saddle of a horse, the hull of a boat.

The reality is that all forms, whether natural or man-made, are subject to the same forces, which we call the forces of nature. In engineering terms the principle is expressed as a 'diagram of forces' and appropriate calculations are made to counteract the distorting forces in buildings, bridges and other structures. While a perfect sphere is the ideal form for a minute sea-creature subjected to equal pressure from all sides, it will distort when used for oil tanks on the earth if not eccentrically reinforced to counteract the pull of gravity: 'and neither does the raindrop nor the round world retain its primal sphericity . . . gravity will always be at hand to drag or distort our drop or bubble' (Thompson, 1961). From an examination of crystals, cells, spicules, skeletons, horns and tusks, D'Arcy Thompson concluded that all forms, whether living or dead, and the *changes in form* required to accommodate growth or movement, could be described in terms of the action of forces. He noticed, in a microscopic examination of bone from a vulture's wing, that it revealed a remarkable similarity to a common engineering structure called a Warren's truss. But the natural form is different in two important ways: it is three-dimensional and it incorporates variations of thickness and angle, each perfectly suited to the function of the part in its relationship to the whole.

(Stevens, 1976)

Patterns of assembly

Patterns of assembly are a basic method of growth, and the geometry of assembly is the basis of building – its forms literally the building blocks of civilization. The principle is elegantly expressed in crystals. Hexagons will fit together to fill the space with all their edges touching on a flat surface, but on their own they can never enclose curved space: for that pentagons are necessary. Pentagons define the forms of most flowers, but none of the crystals, of which there are seven systems only. For the complete enclosure of three-dimensional space by means of regular geometric forms, only five regular polyhedrons can be produced. Such are the limitations of space and form (Stevens, 1976). It is of course possible to mix shapes to produce other forms, but these themselves are subject to strict limitations depending upon the number of sides, their length, and the angles between them. Apart from the strange geometry of crystals, nature has devised other, more organic methods of combining elements. These include the packing of growing units such as the grains of a maize cob, the segments of a pineapple, and the shell of a tortoise. Although basically regular in form, they illustrate the advantage of the hierarchical principle of units being grouped to form larger and larger wholes. Overlapping is a variation on the method, used in plant forms such as pine-cones, and the scales of fish and reptiles.

Both systems have been followed in traditional building, the first in walls and paving, the second in roofing with slates and tiles. Examples of the first occur at their most 'organic' in the ancient stone walling found in parts of South America and Greece, which have earned the name Cyclopean. The second is still common on buildings in many parts of Europe. Especially remarkable are the scale-like surfaces achieved by skilled slaters to emphasize the curves of church and chateaux towers in France and Germany. Apart from building in mud, it is in the combination of such hand-crafted techniques as these into a unified whole that we come nearest to the idea of the building as an organism. The same applies to paving. But the scope of paving is greater. Not only can it express the qualities of material and craftsmanship, but it guides – even controls – our movements; moreover it is continuous.

The urban vernacular

In our enthusiasm for the vernacular we forget that paved roads were a rarity until well beyond the end of the eighteenth century, and that most of the paving in our towns and cities is a product of the Industrial Revolution. The concentration of wealth devoted to industrial and civic buildings gave an enormous boost to the building trades, and industry provided machinery for quarrying and transport for materials. The result was that the streets and footpaths of towns and cities all over Britain were paved with granite and York stone.

Similar traditions developed elsewhere in Europe, giving identity to particular places. There are distinct differences between the paving of Berlin (Norberg-Schulz, 1980), Paris, London and Rome; with specific design innovations, for example, using geometrical progressions, in Marburg (Lancaster, 1984). Innovation is necessary to every tradition to keep it alive; but there must not be too much. The practical problem today is to reconcile the need for order with the need for variety: 'the most basic fact of aesthetic experience [is] the fact that delight lies somewhere between boredom and confusion' (Gombrich, 1984).

Gombrich evokes the analogy of the work-song, which combines the regularity essential for rhythmical movement with occasional variations to lift the participants from the threshold of boredom. Monotony bores us; but equally, so does excessive novelty or variety. This common failing in today's urban environments will easily confuse our already over-stimulated senses, and cause us to lose interest and give up. We are not tempted to analyse the average example of crazy-paving, but the controlled hierarchy of a Medieval church pavement will hold and repay our attention. 'The very ease of reconstruction allows us to go on and enjoy that unity in complexity that has always appealed to paviors and other pattern-makers' (Gombrich, 1984).

To address the problem effectively we need to look much further than traditional patterns and materials to the ever-present urban realities of signs, advertising, lighting, traffic bollards, and white and yellow lines. All are subject to 'codes of practice', but only very rarely are they co-ordinated into the design of cities. They are all now a part of the urban vernacular; just as the shacks of 'bidonvilles' have a claim for consideration as the vernacular dwellings of the twentieth century (Turan, 1982).

Organic engineering

Contemporary architects and engineers are beginning to achieve much more organic forms with their large structures. The Sydney Opera House is an obvious example, reputedly inspired by sections of orange peel, others are tent structures, calculated with computer models based upon soap-bubble membranes. It is also possible to achieve a semblance of organic form using assemblies of small parts, applying the principle of craftsmanship to machine products – as in the case of Nicholas Grimshaw's Channel Tunnel terminal snaking its way along the platforms of Waterloo. The principles behind Buckminster Fuller's geometric structures are also organic. The Montreal dome is composed of hexagons complemented by pentagons, which – if it were formed into a complete sphere – would number precisely twelve. Nature's equivalent is the shell of a minute unicellular organism, *Aulonia hexagona*, which is like a simple mathematical figure. But its hexagons are not quite regular, nor do they make a rigidly definable pattern, but rather a rhythm which depends equally upon the differences involved in each exhibition of the pattern (Waddington, 1968).

These large buildings can be seen to respond to two aesthetic principles: that applying to the natural or organic, and that applying to the geometric, which we usually but misguidedly associate only with the artificial, defined by the Greek Theory of Forms:

I will try to speak of the beauty of shapes, and I do not mean, as most people would suppose, the shapes of living figures, or their imitations in painting, but I mean straight lines and curves and the shapes made from them, by the lathe, ruler or square. They are not beautiful for any particular reason or purpose, as other things are, but are eternally, and by their very nature beautiful, and give a pleasure of their own quite free from the itch of desire; and in this way colours can give a similar pleasure.

(Spoken by Socrates in the Philebus of Plato, Clark, 1961).

Kenneth Clark wrote with some regret that the influence of the latter had gone into engineering rather than art, quoting Marinetti's description of a racing car: 'its frame adorned with great pipes, like snakes with explosive breath, a roaring motor car that seems to be running on shrapnel, is more beautiful than the Victory of Samothrace.' (Clark, 1961). The idea of a machine composed of Platonic forms would have pleased Socrates, as it pleased Le Corbusier. There is an interesting parallel in the forms of tribal sculpture, which exerted such a strong influence on Picasso and Brancusi. But the tribal sculptor was not so exclusive: it is possible, in West African sculpture, to find many examples of the use of both kinds of form, the organic and the geometric. Both, of course, are fundamentally natural.

A great failure of modernism is the cultural specialization which gives us such blinkered views of the world, limiting our vision to a few specialisms which inhibit understanding of the fundamental role of nature and natural forces. Its success was in getting rid of the baggage of romanticism which impaired that vision. Now that we are beginning to get a clear view of the nature of the environment, both in the global sense and in the sense of our own immediate surroundings, we can start to look forward to the future.

1.5 Landscape architecture

Landscape means more than scenery painting, a pleasant rural vista, or ornamental planting around a country house. It means shaped land, land modified for perma-

nent human occupation, for dwelling, agriculture, government, worship, and for pleasure. A landscape happens not by chance, but by contrivance, by premeditation, by design.

(J.R. Stilgoe, *Common Landscape of America 1580–1845*)

Until the nineteenth century there was no clear professional distinction between the designers of houses and gardens. Lancelot Brown ran a successful architectural practice, later inherited by Henry Holland, although clearly his main efforts were devoted to the 'scenic architecture' by which he made his name. Landscape gardening, like architecture, was learned through experience with practitioners, using the great gardens of the past as models. Brown, uniquely, saw his models around him in 'the relics of agriculture and industry: from the enclosure of commons, from hedgerows and boundary trees, from the serpentine lakes created to power watermills' (Elliott, 1986), which, in a sense, he purified through the aesthetic theories of Burke and Hogarth, seeking to recreate nature and her materials in their ideal perfected forms. Neither he, nor his mentor and predecessor Kent, left much in the way of texts; the examples were in his work, which, by the time of his death in 1783, was losing favour. The rich and aristocratic clients that had supported an establishment culture were already beginning to be displaced by a new gardening public with different requirements, which his successors could more effectively fulfil. Where Brown had offered only one solution, Humphry Repton offered options in any one of many styles to suit the client's own individual taste (Dixon-Hunt, 1993).

An Association for the Encouragement of Gardening was set up by Peter Josef Lenné (1789–1866) in Germany in 1822, followed in 1824 by a Gardening School and Provincial Tree Nursery. Also in 1822, John Claudius Loudon (1783–1843) assisted by his wife Jane, published *The Encyclopaedia of Gardening*. This was a comprehensive work of 1400 pages, dealing with the subject from the historical, technical, aesthetic and horticultural points of view, gathered from his experience and observations in a number of tours he had made to visit the great gardens of Europe. His views on the education of the gardener included moral, religious and intellectual needs, as well as physical education. As the son of a farmer, and a prolific writer and editor, he expressed his views on all aspects of the landscape, including farming, forestry, public parks – several of which he designed – and civic squares. Towards the end of his life he established two periodicals, which ran in parallel – *The Gardener's Magazine* and *The Architectural Magazine*.

The term landscape architecture seems to have been used first by the traveller Gilbert Meason to describe a style of building found in Italian landscape paintings. It was used by A.J. Downing to describe rural architecture, and adapted subsequently by Olmsted and Vaux as a professional title appropriate to their competition submission for Central Park, New York in 1857. In 1904 it was taken up by Patrick Geddes, the biologist and planner, after a visit to the Boston Parks. In submitting his design for a new system of parks in Dunfermline, Scotland, he called himself a Landscape Architect (Turner, 1987).

Teaching began in England with the appointment of another planner, Thomas Mawson, as university lecturer in Landscape Architecture to the Department of Civic Design in Liverpool – the university which had pioneered architecture as an academic discipline in 1894. The profession was formally established in 1929 by a group of architects, planners and garden designers, as the British Association of Garden Architects, a name which, after only two months, was changed to the Institute of Landscape Architects (ILA). The distinction is significant, indicative of the professional bias of the founder members, among whom were the architects, Hill, Jellicoe, Jenkins and Parker, heralding the direction which the profession was to follow. The first full-time course in England was started about 1932, at the University of Reading. This was a three-year undergraduate course taught mainly in the Department of Horticulture, but as a cross-faculty course between the Faculty of Agriculture and the Faculty of Letters, with some teaching in the School of Fine Art – indicative, perhaps, of the peculiarly English way in which the profession was perceived.

The pattern of development in other parts of Europe was similar, although the institutions and academic affiliations varied considerably. Some were private, some were part-time, and some were service courses to other disciplines. There were courses in Poland, Switzerland, Denmark, Germany, Holland, Sweden and Turkey, between the end of the First World War and the early 1930s. Professional institutes soon followed. The common title was Garden Architecture, reflecting the character of much of the work, but this has gradually been dropped in favour of Landscape Architecture.

The need for reconstruction after the Second World War prompted the development of further courses, a process which was hastened by the foundation of IFLA – the International Federation of Landscape Architects – in 1956. By the 1980s there were fifty European courses listed in the IFLA Report on Education (1981). These included one each in Austria, Bulgaria, Finland, France, Germany (DDR), Hungary, Italy, Norway, Poland, Sweden, Turkey and Yugoslavia. The Netherlands, Portugal and Switzerland had two each, Denmark three, and Britain and West Germany each had eleven.

The duration of the courses varied between two years postgraduate study, three years undergraduate degree or diploma, and three plus one or two years leading to a degree with diploma, with postgraduate studies added as appropriate. The types of schools varied widely, as did the course content and the nature of the qualification. Diploma Ing. (Engineering) was common in Germany and the German-speaking countries, usually referring to a high input of science-based courses, like the parallel courses in German schools of architecture. In Britain, both Architecture and Landscape Architecture are traditionally arts-based courses, and the latter has been established almost exclusively in schools of architecture or planning, reflecting the professional links that had developed. Several of these were originally also associated with the fine arts, including one which began as a remarkable attempt to unite the disciplines of Architecture, Landscape (Architecture) and Planning, on vaguely Bauhaus lines, with Painting, Sculpture and Fashion Design. As a corporate enterprise it failed because of professional pressures, lack of co-operation between the 'fine' and the 'applied' arts, and want of resources. For many years there was only one British course based upon land sciences – a common characteristic of courses on the European mainland – but that situation is beginning to change.

Courses generally have developed in arrears of perceived demand, subject as they are to the constraints of the educational establishment – finance, staff availability, academic support and employment possibilities. Typically, the earliest courses were history based, with a variable content of design, horticulture, technical studies and materials. Design Theory and Practice were key subjects, but Ecology, Landscape Management and Landscape Planning were not much taught before the war. Now they have become key subjects in many courses, and some professional institutes have established separate classes of membership to accommodate them. The functions covered by the first two are clear, but that of Landscape Planning is ambivalent, usually – and inadequately – being regarded as a function of Town Planning which relates more to Architecture than to Landscape Architecture.

While design traditions and, to some extent, practitioners have always crossed borders, the theoretical basis for landscape design and education has been determined largely by language and national culture. The Scandinavian countries and Finland have been drawn together in their isolation, and to Germany via Denmark for their links with the European mainland, and Germany has natural linguistic connections with Austria and part of Switzerland. Both Luxembourg and Belgium have been culturally divided, while The Netherlands, France, Britain and the Mediterranean countries have remained relatively segregated from one another until recently; and the countries of the Eastern bloc have been segregated politically. The picture that emerges, insofar as it is possible to generalize, is one in which both education and practice are still divided at the professional level, between the architectural and the natural – the old dichotomy. There are, however, encouraging signs. Increasing contacts between schools in different countries with student exchanges are revealing both common objectives and important areas of specialization that can be developed for mutual benefit. Whether there are desirable objectives in common for the landscapes of the twenty-first century, is a subject that has not been fully addressed.

If we discount the retreat into the past, there are currently two trends – cultural plurality and critical regionalism. Ease of communication makes the first inevitable – it is unstoppable. Also it offers exciting possibilities. Critical regionalism demands more care and a greater subtlety of approach. In this, landscape designers have a lead over architects in the primacy of natural habitats. But it is clear that that alone is not enough. As our countries move closer and closer together in terms of trade, political systems, society and education, there is a clear reaction of nationalism and regionalism. Where better can that be expressed than in the natural distinctions of the landscape and its buildings?

CHAPTER 2

Nature rediscovered

Nature does more than supply materials;
she also supplies powers.
(John Stuart Mill)

The involvement with nature came initially from the outside: first in concern for dwindling natural resources, then with the use of native plants, and finally in the creation of habitats. Concern over the human erosion of the wilderness areas of North America, much celebrated by writers such as Thoreau, Twain and Muir, led the 'back-to-nature' enthusiasts to combine in an unlikely alliance with hunters, gun-manufacturers, foresters and conservationists, to campaign for some degree of control, which would include Public Rights of Access. The result was legislation (1864) for Yosemite Valley and the Big Tree Groves, the appointment of Frederick Law Olmsted as a commissioner, and the eventual establishment of the American National Parks Service (1914) (Hunter, 1985; Tischler, 1989).

The principle of conservation was later adapted by Jens Jensen, who became associated with Frank Lloyd Wright and 'the Prairie Style', and developed the use of indigenous plants in his work as superintendent of Chicago Parks. In England, it had been adopted by the gardening writer William Robinson (1838–1935) when faced with the problem of finding plants hardy enough for the changes in the English climate. The publication of *The Wild Garden* in 1870 sparked off a revolution in gardening practice, which, with the ideas expressed in *The English Flower Garden* (1883), had a direct influence on Gertrude Jekyll, who began experimenting with colour (see Natural colour section). Both were a stimulus to the development of a natural approach on the European mainland – particularly in the '*heem*' parks of Jacques P Thijsse and, less directly, in the Stockholm parks and their successors.

Such designed 'natural' landscapes as the *heem* parks require considerable specialized management, both for

arresting the natural plant succession to sustain visual interest and to accommodate human intrusion. This has led to a variety of experiments, ranging from public maintenance on some housing estates to more natural uses of plant communities. At Madestein in The Hague (1982) a phyto-sociological garden has been developed to accord precisely with the surrounding habitats and, also in Holland, experiments have been conducted on the basis of laboratory studies of soil and water, with the objective of producing self-maintaining gardens (Ruff, 1986). Some degree of public participation has now become almost obligatory to ensure appreciation, and survival, of public parks. The planting of trees by schoolchildren – for long a common practice in the parklands surrounding Russian housing blocks – has been substituted in many places by sponsored gardening, the broadcasting of seeds, and encouraging natural regeneration. Many designers have commented on the need 'to educate the client', and in some cases, such as the Hafeninsel in Saarbrücken, steps were taken to ensure that the users understood the design intentions.

A relatively recent development is the employment of large-scale engineering techniques to create hills or even 'mountains'. There are precedents for the green hill among the houses at Vaerebroparken (see Natural colour section) in prehistoric and Viking earthworks, but the range of 'mountains' formed with the rubble of bombed buildings, in the Olympiapark, Munich, constitutes an entirely new kind of created landscape. Clearly neither is a copy of nature, but both skilfully and subtly extend nature into the realm of design. The skyline of the latter is contrived to echo and complement the tented profiles of the buildings, and the scale is exaggerated by the selection and disposition of trees. A similar illusionist technique has been employed by the use of small trees for woodlands seen from the viewpoint adjoining the centre of Milton Keynes (see p.70). The resources that can be devoted to such projects from government, industry and sport, can ensure ambitious development and management, including areas in which wildlife is encouraged. This is the case with the Garden Exhibitions in Germany (*Gartenschauen*) and Holland, where they are the subject of long-term planning, both for their preparation and in their after-use and management. In Germany the local, provincial and national *Gartenschauen* have played a key role in the restructuring of urban open space since the war. Conversely, much of the effort and enterprise devoted to the British Garden Exhibitions has been dissipated by poor planning and an over-reliance on market forces.

The use of technology has recently been extended beyond the requirements of land reclamation from the sea and plant breeding for effect, into the areas of artificially sustained 'natural' environments and as a remedy for pollution. Control of light, nutrients, water and even the creation of artificial soil have become relatively common features of urban landscapes such as the 'hanging' roof gardens of Basingstoke, the Broadgate development in London and Stockley Park – all expensive projects achieved by co-operation between private industry and government. The last, a combined 'industrial park', golf course and park for public recreation, sited on the old town rubbish tip, involved a complete restructuring of soil and landscape after the removal of the rubbish-polluted soil. Recent research into the problem of soil pollution has revealed the value of certain plants in absorbing metals. These 'hyper-accumulators' are capable of storing several times more metal than 'normal' species. For example, the latex in one species, *Sebertia acuminata*, a native of metal-rich soils, can be as much as 11 per cent nickel. The testing of ten plant species on a site contaminated with a 20-year accumulation of London industrial sludge revealed an absorption of zinc, copper, manganese and cadmium. Research concluded that three species – a close relative of alyssum, an alpine penny cress and northern rock cress – all have an unusually large capacity for storing metals (Watts, 1993).

Experiments in air and climate control are notoriously difficult to measure, but there is clear evidence from the scientific studies of trees by Dr A. Bernatsky. He calculated that an average beech tree, 25 m high with a crown diameter of 15 m, could convert 2400 g of carbon dioxide (CO_2) – that is the CO_2 content of 5000 m^3 of air, or the volume of ten houses – per hour under average conditions. It would also use 960 g of water and 6075 calories of sunlight, producing 1600 g of glucose and 1712 g of oxygen. A tree 100 years old will have consumed the carbon dioxide of 800 homes annually, or two homes per day (Bernatsky, 1969). Such vital information must be widely publicized to support the landscape policies for the future.

2.1 Veerse Meer, Oosterschelde, Zeeland, The Netherlands

Nico de Jonge and Ellen Brandes: Staatsbosbeheer (Government Forest Agency).

The Verse Meer (Verse City Lake) was created by closing the sea branch of the Veerse Gat, a part of the delta works (*Deltawerken*) designed to protect the province of Zeeland against flooding. The dangerous sea branch was transformed into a sheltered sweet-water lake, offering new possibilties for nature conservation and active recreation. An important design consideration was the zoning of activities, including water traffic, the provision of shelter to reduce the wind erosion of the shores and the design of new islands with woodland cover. The form of the islands reflects the shallow depth of the water (average 1 m) and the natural forms of the tidal landscape. The woodland pattern is deliberately geometrical to contrast with them. The woodlands are spatially linked to define the zones, those parts reserved for nature having a more open character.

The Verse Meer woodland (*Veersebos*) was planted at the beginning of the 1950s as part of the restoration of Walcheren, which had been flooded by bombing in the last year of the war, causing natural creeks to be formed. The ambitious plans of the forest agency were, however, modified, resulting in only 30 hectares of woodland together with some agricultural land. The design problem was to integrate the new woodlands, the rectilinear fields and the flowing lines of the creeks.

Figure 2.1 Veerse Meer

▼ (i) The plan shows the contrast between the 'natural' water areas and the geometry of woodlands and fields

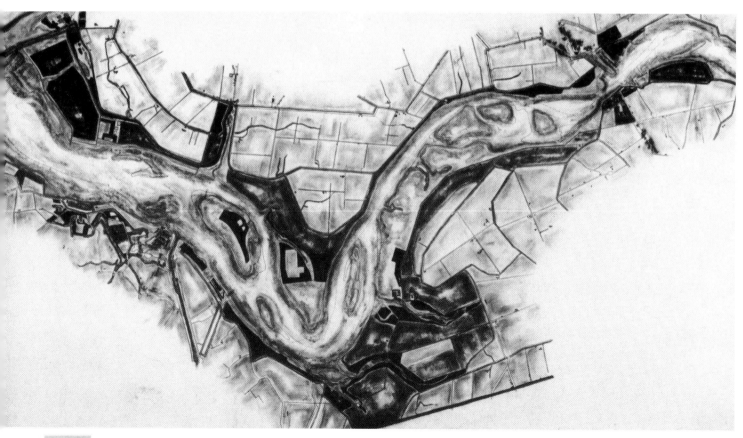

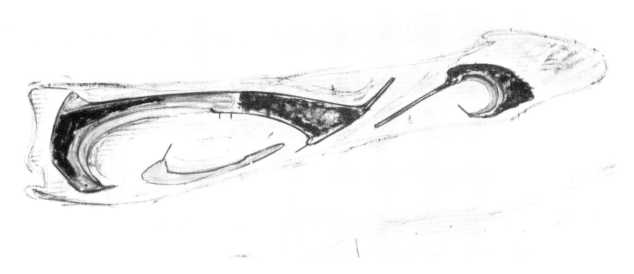

▲ (ii) New 'organic' island as proposed

◄ (iii) Island as constructed

▼ (iv) The contrast between the natural and man-made patterns

▼ (v) Woodland path with typical brick paving laid in sand

2.2 Ruissalo, Turku, Finland 1986–9

Virve Veistera: City of Turku

In 1986 the City of Turku commissioned a management and land-use plan for a site of 845 ha on the island of Ruissalo. The island is 7 km long and 1 km wide, and is linked by a bridge to the old city, which was until 1812 capital of Finland. In the sixteenth century it was a Royal hunting park and in the nineteenth century it became a popular retreat when about 50 wooden villas were built to relate to beaches and dancing pavilions. Now the island is an important recreation area, with a large part devoted to nature conservation. The flourishing woodlands of limes (*Tilia cordata*) and oaks (*Quercus robur*) in the north-eastern part contrast with the poorer woodlands of the dryer south-west, which are regarded as having a southern exotic flavour. In this area there is a large holiday hotel with a harbour for sailing boats and a camp-site. The most important objective of the project was to preserve the unique character both of the natural landscape and the historical elements, which are threatened by large-scale modern developments.

Figure 2.2 Ruissalo

▼ (i) Landscape management plan showing various types of forest habitat with lists of plant communities and tourist facilities

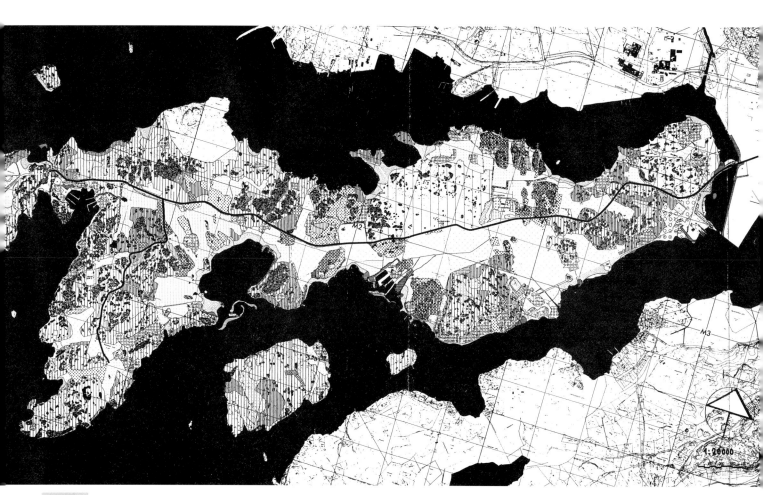

► (ii) This white-painted nineteenth century villa contrasts with the surrounding woodland

◄ (iii) Informal woodland path

2.3 The Heemparks of Amstelveen, Amsterdam, The Netherlands

C. P. Broerse

The Amsterdam peatlands in which the new township of Amstelveen is situated presented a particular challenge to the designers of the parks in the 1930s and 1940s. C.P. Broerse saw the opportunity to design a park that was inspired by the natural and semi-natural landscape using the native plant species that still existed at the time. With the nutrient-poor soil as a starting point, different habitats could be created, using a variety of plants that rarely occurred in public parks. The aim was not so much to imitate nature but to design with nature, making creative use of natural surroundings and wild plants. Composition and spatial effects were deliberately exploited to emphasize the natural character. It was an innovative approach that resulted in De Braak park (1939), the Jacques Thijssepark (1941) and others of similar type. Characteristically, curving pathways lead through woodland with flowery verges, and intimate spaces alternate with views over water enhanced by moorland vegetation and groups of trees. Flowing lines are typical and generally the atmosphere of the parks is one of silence and natural harmony. The planted areas are, however, in essence, dynamic – much more so than those of cultivated park plants, and they present particular problems for management. Apart from traditional methods of maintenance, the heem parks demand ecological knowledge, observation and judgement, creative vision and considerable experience, presupposing long-term planning and specialized professional management.

In Amstelveen, a type of landscape has been developed that represents a new direction for the profession, demanding a creatively flexible approach. The designer is required, not only to compose artificial landscapes, but to make – and combine them with – natural habitats, as well as predicting the long-term effects.

2.4 Olympiapark, Munich, Germany 1972

Günther Grizmek: Landscape Architect

The designer's intention was to transform the dull flatlands of northern Munich into a new landscape of lakes and hills for a 'Green Olympics'. But it was not to be a copy of nature; rather an imitation of nature in an architectonically conceived composition combining land-form, buildings, water and plants. The buildings – stadium, athletics and swimming areas – were seen, not as separate monumental structures, but integrated by the overriding tent roofs within the 150 ha public park.

The 'mountain' began with a pile of rubble from the bombed city. From this and from some excavation and landfill it was possible to create a range of artificial hills up to 60 m high, overlooking a lake retained by a dam 8 m high and extending for several hundred metres. This dominant man-made feature offers panoramic views over the Olympic site to the north and across the city to the south. It also generates the different levels of circulation between pedestrians and motorized traffic which extend over the whole site; special care was taken to design the sixteen pedestrian overpasses in such a way that their lines are integrated with the topography. The lake which separates the public park from the sports buildings, the

College for Physical Education, the Olympic Village and the tennis courts, is fed by the Nymphenburger Canal. As the bottom is 3 m higher than the level of the ground in the stadium, it has been sealed with fine asphaltic concrete laid over plastic fabric.

The planting strategy echoes the design strategy. The large scale of the land-forms, robust planting and the avoidance of ornamental plants, have rendered fencing unnecessary. The steep slopes of the hills have been planted with resilient mountain pine (*Pinus montana mughus*), dwarf oak (*Quercus sessilis*) and wild roses – all chosen for their small scale to exaggerate the scale of the hills; and the summits have been left bare. The lakeside has been planted with white willow (*Salix alba*), and the promenades and footpaths with lime trees (*Tilia verschidina*) – both native to Munich – and traffic and border areas have been planted with ash (*Fraxinus excelsior*) and Norway maple (*Acer platanoides*). Small-scale planting includes a wild-flower 'mountain pasture', a water-meadow with reed-grass and marsh marigolds, lakeside water-plants and hardy edge planting around areas of intensive use.

Figure 2.4 Olympiapark

▼ (i) 'Natural' tent shapes covering the stadium relate closely to the organic forms of the lake and hills

▼ (ii) The need for an environment secluded from traffic and buildings can be seen from this plan

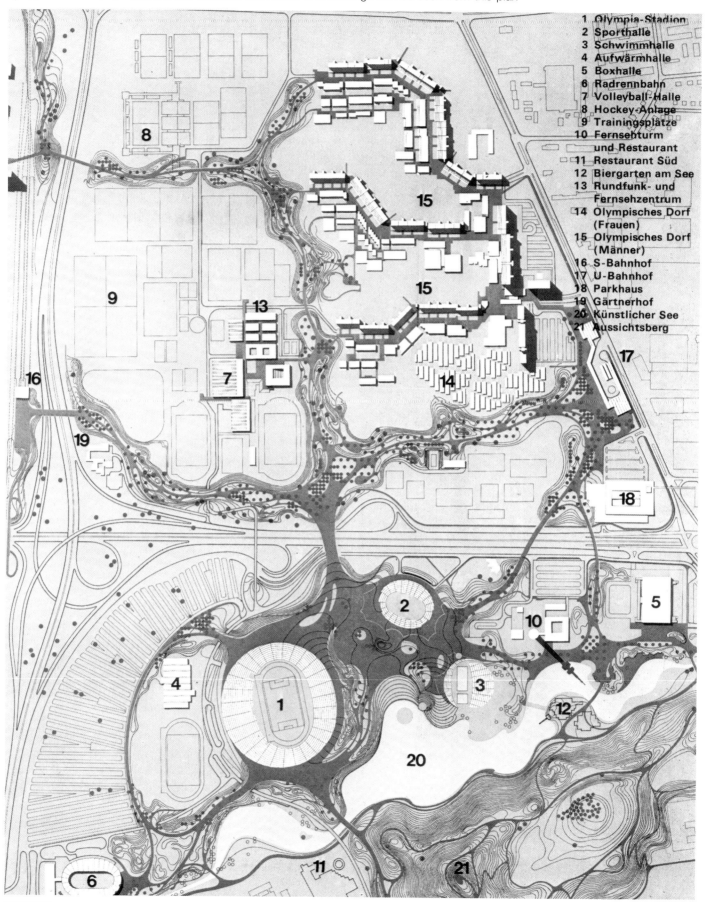

1 Olympia-Stadion
2 Sporthalle
3 Schwimmhalle
4 Aufwärmhalle
5 Boxhalle
6 Radrennbahn
7 Volleyball-Halle
8 Hockey-Anlage
9 Trainingsplätze
10 Fernsehturm
   und Restaurant
11 Restaurant Süd
12 Biergarten am See
13 Rundfunk- und
   Fernsehzentrum
14 Olympisches Dorf
   (Frauen)
15 Olympisches Dorf
   (Männer)
16 S-Bahnhof
17 U-Bahnhof
18 Parkhaus
19 Gärtnerhof
20 Künstlicher See
21 Aussichtsberg

◀ (iii) View of 'mountain' from paved area with semi-mature trees

◀ (iv) Approach to stadium from hills by granite sett path

▲ (v) The scale of the artificial hills appears to be increased by the use and arrangement of small-scale planting; their skyline echoes that of the tented stadium

◀ (vi) View across hill to housing and allotments; serpentine paths exaggerate the scale

2.5 Hafeninsel,
Saarbrücken, Germany

Latz and Partner

The island river port of Saarbrücken was destroyed during the war, and in the rebuilding of the city the docks were filled. It was not until the mid-seventies that open-space planning began to be seen as a viable alternative to the proposals for a mini-Manhatten, but not before a motorway with slip-roads and bridges had been constructed, bisecting the site. Three alternatives were suggested: the first two comprised different styles of landscape park, informal and formal. Both involved clearing the site and obliterating the relics of industry. The third alternative argued the case for a new approach which combined the traces of the past with present requirements, and anticipating the future, thereby expressing the continuity of history. This integrated approach to design required the establishment of new and unfamiliar mechanisms within the local authority, initially to enable implementation, and subsequently to ensure continued planting and maintenance would take place effectively.

Old structures were carefully uncovered; some were retained and used to determine the pattern of development. Visual links were established both within the site and to surrounding buildings, suburbs and hills – emphasizing the designer's acceptance of the present – and the river has been made visible. High-level railway and gantry structures and other remains have provided the basis for the design of walls, pergolas and steps, which are intended to emphasize the established nature of the park. This theme is continued in the encouragement of

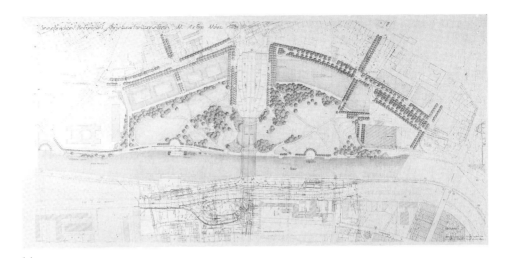

(a)

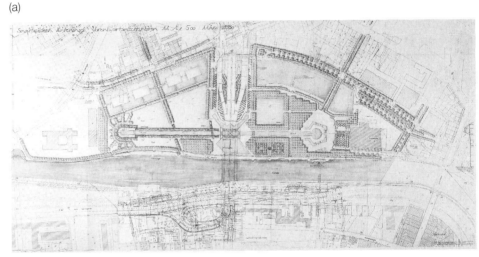

(b)

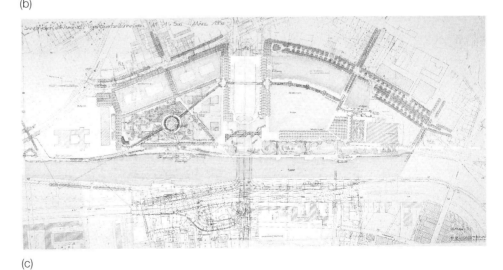

(c)

Figure 2.5 Hafeninsel
(i) Design process plans (a) the natural approach; (b) the formal approach; (c) the integrated approach

vegetation, which includes natural plants, garden escapes plus the exotics carried in by ships in the past. Local involvement in sowing seeds, gardening and general maintenance is encouraged. Having rejected the first two 'traditional' designs, the landscape architect and the people of the city, supported by the city authorities, have embarked upon a new kind of developing landscape, which combines some of the features of industrial archaeology with those of landscape design and implementation to achieve an effective collaboration.

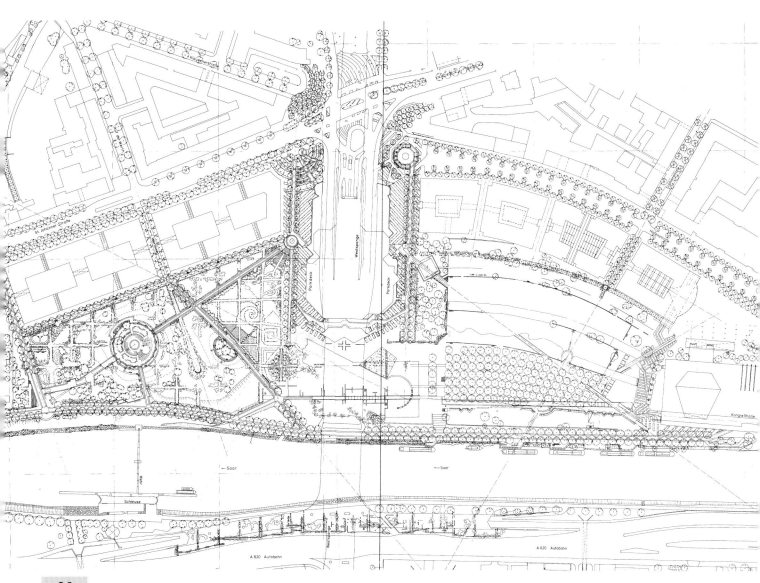

(iii) The water wall is both functional and symbolic; symbolizing 'the town in ruins', it also serves to oxygenate the water in the pool

▼ (iv) Principal paths

▼ (v) Theatre with chestnut grove

◀ (vi) Rotunda with gardens

▼ (vii) 'Natural' area of wildflowers

▼ (viii) Detail of wall with water-spout

2.6 University of Zürich – Irchel: Western Park, Switzerland

Eduard Neuenschwander

The design of the Western Park was the subject of a public competition in 1978 (together with the Northern Park which was awarded to architects Gerwin Engel and Klaus Holzhausen). The site, including the Sports Centre, comprises 12 ha out of a total of 45 ha of university land. It lies in a valley between the city centre and the suburbs, with links to the Zurich and Waldberg forested hills.

The main objective was to create a multi-use space which would harmonize with the whole environment, catering for the needs of the university and public. These include active sports, children's playgrounds, and areas for passive recreation.

Major excavations were undertaken, including the disposal of 400 000 m³ of earth and large quantities of building rubble, in the creation of a lake, and mounding to act as a buffer against traffic noise. The lake is the core of the park. It is carefully edged with stone and wood structures, protecting the banks and providing safe play areas for children. The lake and the

Figure 2.6 University of Zurich – Irchel

▼ (i) Natural vegetation at the edge of the lake

surrounding area of land act as natural biotopes. Horticultural planting has been avoided in favour of hardy wild plants growing in the untreated soil of the site. The strong emphasis on natural solutions helps to stimulate an awareness of nature and evokes a sense of freedom, which effectively reduces aggression and vandalism.

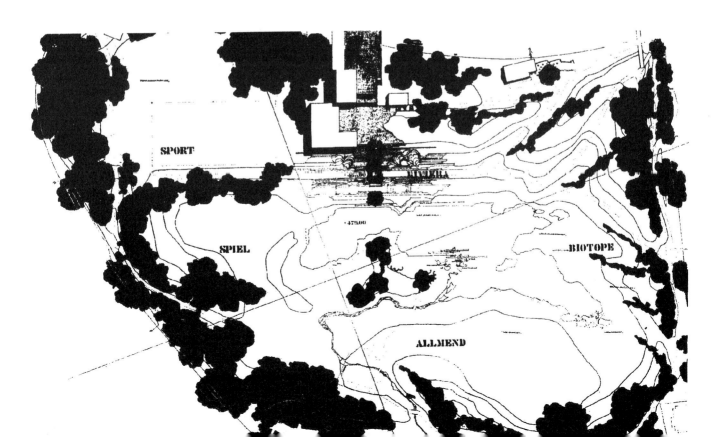

▲ (iii) Granite setts, riven sandstone slabs and timber decking

▲ (iv) A landscape of stone steps at the lake edge

▼ (ii) Materials have been arranged specifically to exploit the different qualities of form, texture and colour

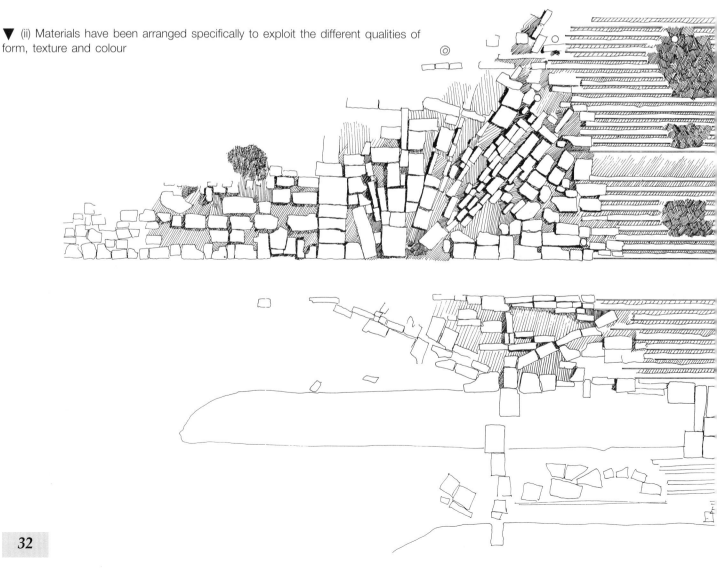

▲ (v) Natural boulders and gravel contrasted with patterns of stone paving

▲ (vi) Play area with stepped stone bridge

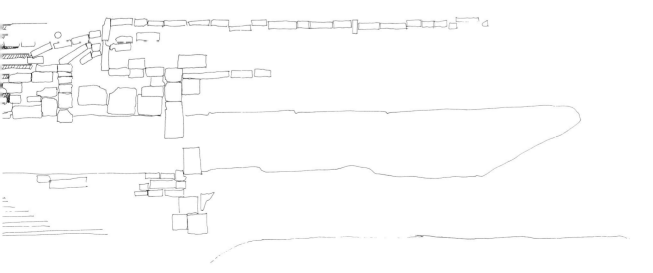

NATURAL COLOUR

Colour depends upon three variables – light, surface and distance – each one of which is within our control. Most obviously, we can control the surface: in terms of size, orientation or alignment, and pigmentation. Both the walls of buildings and paved surfaces act as giant reflectors, absorbing some of the wavelengths of light and returning others as colour. They are often the cause of glare: a good reason to exercise caution when introducing any large smooth surfaces into the environment, which itself is naturally textured. Apart from those of water, surfaces in nature are rarely smooth and never simple. This applies equally to the predominantly mineral surfaces of earth, rock and natural building materials, and to vegetation – although vegetation has its own particular complexity.

The surfaces of vegetation are broken into small reflective units, complicated by the way in which the colours are optically mixed. Not only do they comprise different elements such as bark, buds, flowers and leaves, but they catch the light from different directions, reflecting it in a variety of different ways. It is this, combined with the changes due to growth and movement, that make it such a difficult medium. Although they were prepared to accept colour in the interiors of their houses, the eighteenth-century designers dismissed it as an unstable side-effect in their gardens of form. Interest grew in the nineteenth century with the discovery of exotic plants in the Americas and South Africa, and the possibility of their propagation. This coincided with the development of the idea of the garden as a work of art in its own right – neither a picture nor a part of nature. It was consolidated by the publication of the first major work on colour harmony by M.E. Chevreul (1839), who demonstrated how objective criteria could be applied to all areas in which colour is used, from the design of textiles to that of the garden.

Tempting as it is to think of colour vision having been given to us for the purposes of enjoying rainbows and sunsets, the reality is at once more mundane and more remarkable. In common with that of the primates, reptiles, birds, insects and some fish, it has evolved for survival. It has three basic functions: to capture attention, to transmit information, and to affect the emotions of the viewer. As primates emerged rather late in evolutionary history it seems likely that the early tree-dwelling species moved into an ecological niche already occupied by birds: 'they picked the same fruits, caught the same insects and were in danger of being harmed by the same stings and the same poisons' (Humphrey, 1976). For these, brilliant colour was necessary to make them stand out against the predominantly green background.

Trees and plants are green because the chlorophyll in the leaves absorbs the other wavelengths of coloured light, reflecting green. When the chlorophyll needed for photosynthesis breaks down in the autumn, it allows the pigments based on carotene and other substances to take over before the leaves fall, and the chlorophyll returns to do its work the following spring. Perhaps it is this essential function and the ubiquity of green, coupled with the fact that it is 'easy on the eye', that makes us take it for granted, seeing it rather as a background than as a colour in its own right. The value is demonstrated in the ways in which it can be used to manipulate the light, expressing the passing of time through the day. The 'downland effect' of the artificial hill dominating the housing site in Vaerebroparken near Copenhagen, and the ground modelling at Great Linford, Milton Keynes, are seen first as background landscape features. The greenness becomes apparent in the second case, as a colour in complementary contrast to the red of the brick houses. The camera reminds us, as nothing else can, of the inconstancy of nature, by allowing us to see the same view captured in different lights and in different seasons, which reveal surprising colour differences – as in the Heem parks of Amstelveen.

Colour in plants occurs predominantly in the flowers, where it is heightened by translucency, and in the leaves. This has given rise to two traditions: that of 'carpet-bedding', and that of the herbaceous border. The first has become popular everywhere, having developed into a folk-art depicting heraldic arms and floral clocks with more regard for ingenuity than colour co-ordination. The herbaceous border was developed with great subtlety by Gertrude Jekyll, with spectral sequences, using analogous colours, the use of complementaries and 'advancing and retreating', warm and cold colours, as described by Chevreul. The former 'bedding' technique was adapted by Roberto Burle Marx for his 'painting with plants', and subsequently by the painter Lothar Schall and Büro Luz for the Gartenschau in Baden-Baden: the first using foliage and the second flowers, which are much more vibrant in colour. Striking comparisons can be made between the deliberately discordant – or at least unusual – colour scheme, and the more subtle harmonies in the garden of the painter Ton ter Linden and that of the Blomsterhaven, Lyngby. More commonly, plants are seen in juxtaposition with built surfaces, with which some degree of contrast is usually desirable. The autumnal colour of the climbing plant and the contrasted travertine banding on the curved inner courtyard wall of James Stirling's Staatsgalerie in Stuttgart combine with the shadows to make an elegant composition.

Vaerebroparken, Skovbrynet, Gladsaxe, Denmark (design: Jørn Palle Schmidt, landscape architect; P.E. Hoff and B. Windings, architects).

The grass-covered hill appears as a landmark in the relatively flat countryside, catching the sunlight and acting as an indicator of the passing of time through the day. This is remarkably successful, although changes in the density of housing from that originally envisaged in the design competition have led to problems of drainage

Milton Keynes, Villages Grid Square, Great Linford, UK (design: Michael Lancaster, landscape architect; Martin Richardson, architect).

The light is modulated by ground modelling around the old field drainage ditches. The housing, in traditional red brick, is seen in complementary harmony with the green of the grass – each emphasizes the other to the fullest extent

Staatsgalerie, Stuttgart, Germany (design: James Stirling/Michael Wilford & Associates).

The subtle affinity of colours and textures between the climbing plants and the banded travertine serves to balance the contrasting forms

**Thijssepark, Amstelveen, The Netherlands
(design: C.P. Broerse)**

These three seasonal views capture striking
differences in the relatively subdued natural
palette of this landscape of curving paths
leading through woodland, with flowery verges
opening out into views over water; all based
on the ecology of poor peat soil

Garden Ton ter Linden (design: Ton ter Linden)

The water-colour painter Ton ter Linden compares his method with weaving, creating tensions between waves of colour in which plant stems and foliage play an important role. Like the work of his predecessor, Gertrude Jekyll, it has been described as 'Impressionist' gardening

Blomsterhaven, Lyngby, Denmark (design: Peter Holst and Karen Attwell)

The simple combination of 'advancing' yellow is balanced by the band of 'retreating' purple, both seen against a green background

Landesgartenschau Baden-Baden (design: Luz and Partner, landscape architects; Lothar Schall, painter)

'Painting' with flowers is difficult because of their relatively short life – but the Garden Show/Festival offers ideal opportunities for such experiments. This example was the subject of a unique collaboration between the painter, Lothar Schall and the landscape architects, Luz and Partner. The 'shocking' combinations of colour harmonies and discords recall Schoenberg's observation that musical harmony, with counterpoint and form, is only one of the considerations in musical composition. Arnheim suggests that the principles on which many of the rules of colour harmony are based might be a recipe for dullness 'suitable at best for the so-called colour schemes of clothing or rooms' (Arnheim, 1974). This example of painting with flowers could never be described as dull; but it is probably too exciting to remain for longer than the duration of the exhibition

2.7 The Federal Garden Show 1985, Berlin, Germany

Büro Wolfgang Miller

The natural landscape of Berlin is a product of the last Ice Age. As the glaciers melted some 12 000 years ago they left behind ground moraines which were broken into plateaux by the valleys of the River Spree and the Havel channel. The sandy soil and fertile marls of these plateaux have been farmed for centuries.

The exhibition of 1985 provided an opportunity for a regional park to serve the needs of residents in the suburbs of Neukölln, Kreuzberg, Gropiusstadt, Rudow, Tempelhof and Lichtenrade – all poorly provided with open space – together with those immediately adjacent to Britz, Mariendorf and Buckow, totalling some 600 000 people. From a flat treeless site on old arable land the designers have created, in a remarkably short time, a verdant park with hills, woodlands, lakes and water-meadows. Although originally featureless, the site had

the advantage of an interesting shape, with 'fingers' extending out to different centres of population. In addition it was adjacent to some 3000 allotments, Berlin's largest market garden, a tree nursery and a cemetery. At only one point did buildings actually adjoin the site – and they were low; and it was entirely free from traffic noise. It provided a unique opportunity to create a new regional park.

Water was an obvious requirement. Because clarity was important, it had to be deep, although not as deep as the existing ground water level of 8 m, and a waterproof membrane was necessary. A slight depression on the site suggested the form, and the lake was extended into three arms, with the excavated material forming small hills between them. A formal treatment was adopted for the sides adjoining the entrances – which were conceived as small 'urban' squares – and this was developed as a linear structure to accommodate the detailed elements required by the garden exhibition (*Gartenschau*). The informal, naturalistic treatment of the other sides contributed to the concept of the park as an ecologically viable concept.

Figure 2.7 Federal Garden Show, Berlin
▼ (i) Plan showing 'green' connections to different parts of the city

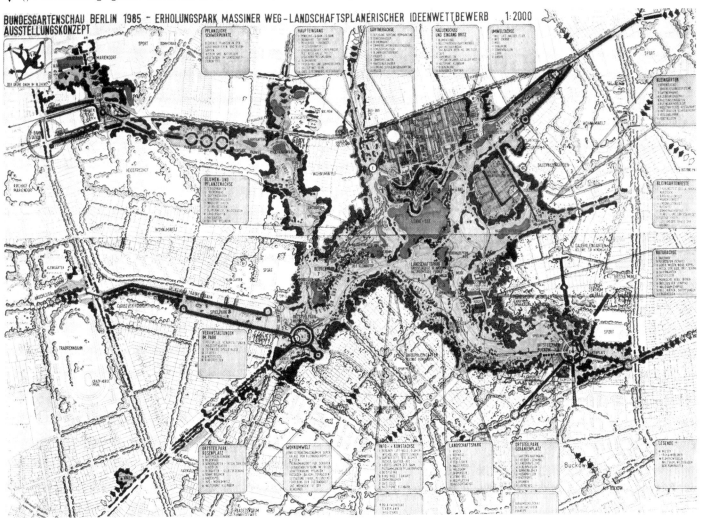

(iii) Wooden bridge over 'mountain stream' ▶

(iv) Lowland stream with willows and water meadows

(v) Oriental effects with trees, rocks, paving and clipped shrubs

2.8 Stuttgart: Design with Climate, 'The Green U', Germany

Stuttgart is an industrial city of 580 000 inhabitants (1992) and the capital city of Baden-Württemberg, home of Mercedes Benz, Porsche and Bosch. It is also a historic city surrounded by wooded hills with orchards and vineyards, within a region of fertile agricultural plains. The steepness of the hills and their liability to subsidence ensured their protection when the industries spread along the valley bottom, separating the city from the river Neckar, which became a ship canal. The

Figure 2.8 'The green U'

(i) Plan of Stuttgart and surroundings showing the links in the chain of 'the green U'. From the central Schlosspark in the south they extend along the main railway line towards the river and Bad Cannstatt, then westwards and northwards, connecting the old zoo and rose garden with the Killesberg quarry park. The site of Expo '93 (see ii) is the final link connecting the old Rosensteinpark and the zoo with the park on the high ground of the Killesberg Quarry and thence to the surrounding countryside.

extyreme difference in altitude, of about 340 m, contributes to its particular charm providing special opportunities for urban and landscape design; it is also the cause of the particular climatic problems associated with 'the city in a hollow'. Inversions have been recorded on about 240 days of the year, often causing air pollution above the critical level.

Design with climate: the Green U

The principle of climatic inversions has long been established, but physical measures to ameliorate them are unusual, if not unique. In the case of Stuttgart they date from 1905, when the authorities were faced with proposals for the expansion of the city up the hills to the north-west. Although house-building was permitted, it was limited to the upper sides of the roads, with gaps between the buildings to allow air-drainage. The 1935 Planning Regulations (*Ortsbausatzung*) were less environmentally orientated, but the subject was taken up again after the war. The ideal was a linked system of open spaces extending from the forests and the vineyards on the hilltops down to the river, which would allow the cool fresh air to flow down at night to displace the warm and polluted air rising from the city and its industries.

Implementation of The Green U, as it came to be called, has taken almost 50 years. Beginning with the existing historic and open spaces, the city authorities have established green links through a series of Garden Shows (*Gartenschauen*), beginning with that designed by Herman Mattern on the wasteland surrounding Killesberg Quarry in 1939, which was extended in 1950. This was followed by others in 1961 and 1977, culminating in that of 1993, to complete the connection. The last, by Hans Luz and Partner, was complicated by a number of road crossings that had been necessitated by the

▲ (ii) IGA 1993 (design: Hans Luz and Partner). The drama of water contrasts with the dark woodland background

▲ (iii) IGA 1993 (design: Hans Luz and Partner). Terraces with 'natural' planting

new road and tramway system linking the outskirts with the city centre. The character of the links is varied, each part being marked by a 'Station' – a resting place typically paved, with fountains, sculptures and plants. The sequence extends from the Schlossplatz in the inner city, via the Upper, Middle and Lower Schlossgarten, to the River Neckar. From there it runs up past the old zoo, through the Rosenstein Park, to the Killesberg Park on the hill, and thence into the surrounding woods and fields.

The city – originally Stutengarten, from *Stute*, a stud-horse – was founded in AD 950 by the Duke of Swabia and it developed as the fortified city of the counts, dukes and, from 1805, the King of Württemberg. The Neues Schloss was started in 1744 and completed as a baroque palace for the king in 1806. The gardens were modernized as part of the 1961 Bundesgartenschau to provide an appropriate focus for shopping, entertainment and cultural activities. A direct pedestrian link was envisaged by the architect James Stirling, in the urban design proposals associated with the adjacent *Staatsgalerie* (Art Gallery). The Upper, Middle and Lower Schlossgarten, which were all parts of the 1961 and 1977 *Bundesgartenschauen*, connect the centre with the river. At this point the roads become predominant, but there are spatial links across to Cannstatt, a compact medieval town with a nineteenth-century spa park, an important source of mineral springs.

Like many old German towns, Stuttgart still suffers from the attempt to make it suit the needs of the automobile – an idea borrowed from North American cities. This was reinforced by the presence of Mercedes Benz, which had arisen from Daimler's invention of the automobile, beside the river in Bad Cannstatt, and also by the urgent post-war need to rebuild the industries and the centre of the medieval city destroyed in the war. A consequence of this spontaneous traffic planning was the division of the Schlossgarten into separate parts, by roads. More importantly, the building of an intersection for a 9-lane and a 6-lane state highway completely dominated the point at which the park met the river. Tunnels were later used to solve the first problem, but the second remains. More recently, controversy has been generated by the building of major roads dominating the valley, and extending as partial viaducts up the hillsides, causing major disturbances to the conserved landscape.

The role of the Gartenschau

The role of the German *Gartenschauen* in restoring and renewing urban open space is perfectly illustrated in Stuttgart. The Bundes or national Garden Shows take place every two years in some part of Germany. Usually they are held as a result of public competitions. But they are rather more than simply garden shows. The commercial exhibition element constitutes a relatively small proportion of the whole investment, which is typically directed towards major long-term landscape improvements. The 1961 *Bundesgartenschau*, based on a concept by Hans Luz and Partners, was focused on the area of the Upper and Middle Schlossgarten. It involved considerable restoration, and the development of the upper area to make it into an effective city centre square. The 1977 show, by Hans Luz, Max Baecher and Diedrich Brunken, closed important gaps by reconnecting the Middle and Lower parts of the Schlossgarten, and the large English-style Rosenstein Park.

The most difficult task for the designers of the 1977 show was to integrate the tramway, a tram-station and turning tracks and to create a new landscape on the top

▼ (iv) Plan of IGA Stuttgart Exp '93

SITE PLAN

WA

KILLESBERG

Ⓑ KILLESBERG
1 Fuchsias
2 Roses
3 Hobby gard
4 Grave plant
  gravestone c
5 Perennials
6 Spring and s
  flowers

of the motorway tunnel. This area is now dominated by the new 'Swan Lake' and the concrete cones of the 'Berger' fountains, spurting jets of symbolic spa-water into the air at intervals. Three new lakes were created, fed by a revived stream, and a completely integrated pedestrian system was established. Intensity of use and the distance from the city centre has been reflected in the use of materials. Continuous surfaces of granite and concrete paving in the centre, give way to discontinuous granite surfaces, and paths in tarmac and woodchip. This is also reflected in the planting, which ranges from close-mown lawns and highly maintained annuals in the centre, to native perennials and wild-flower meadows in the more distant areas. The latter, natural approach was unfamiliar at the time but has since become common throughout Germany.

This approach to the landscape, which is essentially one of *adaptation* – that is, the acceptance of existing landscape assets and the removal of intrusive elements – serves as a model of urban open space development, and a warning against the often inadequately considered 'grand designs'. The fact that it is all a part of the long-term climatic planning, gives it an added validity.

The last and final link in the chain of the Green U was, in a sense, the most difficult. This was to relate the Rosenstein Park to the Killesberg Park, situated about 100 m above the city. The two were separated by roads, a railway corridor, and areas of industry, which had to be bridged to make the final connection. Two small neglected open spaces – an old villa garden and an overgrown orchard on the hillside – facilitated the junction. The Killesberg Park, created by Herman Mattern in an old quarry, has acquired a reputation among German landscape architects for embodying traditional roots. Drystone walls and steps have been carefully integrated with huge areas of perennials, shrubs and parkland trees. It represents the era of landscape gardening based upon arts and crafts

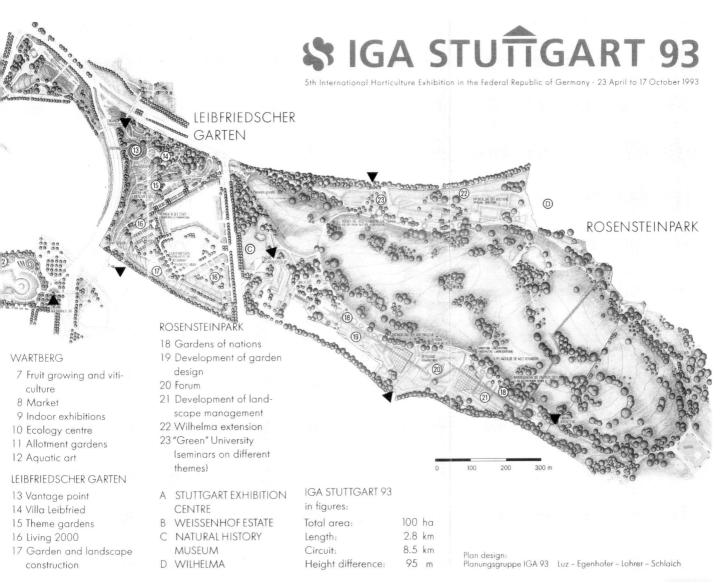

IGA STUTTGART 93

5th International Horticulture Exhibition in the Federal Republic of Germany · 23 April to 17 October 1993

LEIBFRIEDSCHER GARTEN

ROSENSTEINPARK

WARTBERG

7 Fruit growing and viticulture
8 Market
9 Indoor exhibitions
10 Ecology centre
11 Allotment gardens
12 Aquatic art

LEIBFRIEDSCHER GARTEN

13 Vantage point
14 Villa Leibfried
15 Theme gardens
16 Living 2000
17 Garden and landscape construction

ROSENSTEINPARK

18 Gardens of nations
19 Development of garden design
20 Forum
21 Development of landscape management
22 Wilhelma extension
23 "Green" University (seminars on different themes)

A STUTTGART EXHIBITION CENTRE
B WEISSENHOF ESTATE
C NATURAL HISTORY MUSEUM
D WILHELMA

IGA STUTTGART 93
in figures:

Total area: 100 ha
Length: 2.8 km
Circuit: 8.5 km
Height difference: 95 m

Plan design:
Planungsgruppe IGA 93   Luz – Egenhofer – Lohrer – Schlaich

41

▲ (v) IGA 1993 (design: Hans Luz and Partner). A juxtaposition of the formal and the informal

▲ (vi) IGA 1993 (design: Hans Luz and Partner). A diminishing vista of grass steps against a narrowing gap

traditions, before the extensive use of concrete and heavy machines, with design details derived from the vineyards and the villa gardens on the hillsides.

The competition for the 1993 Garden Show was again won by Hans Luz and Partner who led a team of experts including social scientists and ecologists, in addition to the professionals (landscape architects, architects, engineers and artists) who had been employed for the 1977 *Gartenschau*. This was a reflection of current thinking in landscape architecture, which was stated in the theme for the project: 'the responsible treatment of nature in the city'. A special emphasis was placed upon the conservation of rare plants and animals occupying 'ecological niches' in areas of waste ground, also the creation and conservation of private gardens expressing individual attitudes. The potential conflict between nature and public use has been specifically addressed as one of the most pressing problems of our time. Whilst the concept of genuine wilderness is clearly incompatible with the city, contact between people and nature is considered essential and can easily be achieved. This becomes particularly relevant in the light of the fact that the majority of the 50 per cent of all natural species currently endangered in West Germany depend upon traditional methods of land cultivation.

Landscape planners, as heads of multi-disciplinary teams in Stuttgart, are concentrating their attention upon the increasing problem of co-existence between people and nature; in this area of potential conflict there should be no waste land.*

(Compiled from an article by Frieder Luz: 'Stuttgart's Attempt to deal responsibly with Nature in the City' and other sources.)

2.9 Floriade 1992, Zoetermeer, The Netherlands

Michiel den Ruijter, Projectburo Floriade

The fourth national horticultural exhibition (1992) was co-ordinated by national, regional and local, planning authorities to provide a multi-use public park for the new town of Zoetermeer, 10 km east of The Hague. A feasibility study undertaken in 1982 – the year of the previous festival in Amsterdam – led to the selection of a site in the future residential quarter known as Rokkeveen. Zoetermeer was planned as a compact city, with good railway links to The Hague and Germany and good road communications. It is served by a hierar-

chy of parks, of which the exhibition site will constitute one. This park, of 30 ha has been planned to relate both to the new town and the adjacent proposed national forest of 300 ha.

The plan is based upon the traditional *patte d'oie*, but with each axis possessing a different character: the central axis is raised. One advantage is the concentration of the entry points near to the traffic routes and the railway station, congestion being avoided by the even

Figure 2.9 Floriade 1992

▼ (i) Plan showing the dramatic impact of the *patte d'oie* pattern structure of the exhibition park in the polder landscape

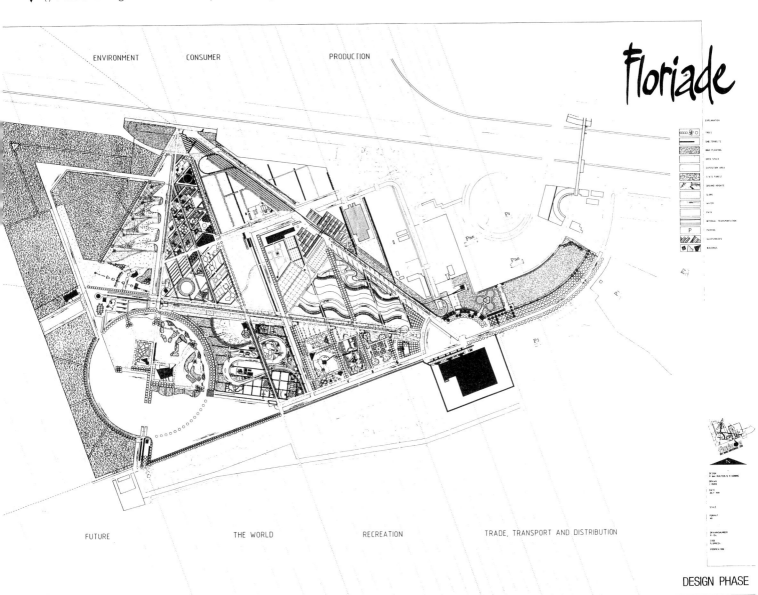

▲ (ii) Main avenue with clipped lime trees showing tree-islands
with weeping willows in the background

distribution of 'honey-pot' facilities throughout the site. Circulation is alternatively direct or meandering, orientation being provided by the straight axes, which are frequently crossed by the meandering ones. The fact that the 25 ha of display area was destined to become residential leaving a permanent park of about 30 ha, meant that park planning and town planning had to be well co-ordinated from the outset. The character of the park was determined by the geometry of the polder landscape, but contained some areas with a natural character, including a lake with reed beds and willow scrub which had low maintenance requirements. The formal parts of the design were much more demanding in terms of layout because of the long straight vistas. To anticipate their effect on site, computer perspectives were generated and used as a basis for artist's renderings, which in turn were used to monitor the design and implementation.

▲ (iii) The middle axis with the monorail running along the top

▲ (iv) The 'wild' Indonesian garden

2.10 Swiss National Sports Centre, Tenero, Switzerland 1988

Paolo L. Bürgi

The site in Tenero, adjoining that of an existing sports centre, was a plateau raised up several metres to avoid flooding from the adjoining lake. The designer has acknowledged two main influences: the pattern of the surrounding landscape which vaguely recalls the Roman practice of *Centuriation*, and the axis of the existing buildings. Accepting and retaining the old patterns of woodland and hedgerows, he superimposed a dominant regular grid of tree-lined avenues with small enclosed squares surrounded by pleached trees and clipped hedges.

Figure 2.10 Swiss National Centre

▼ (i) Plan

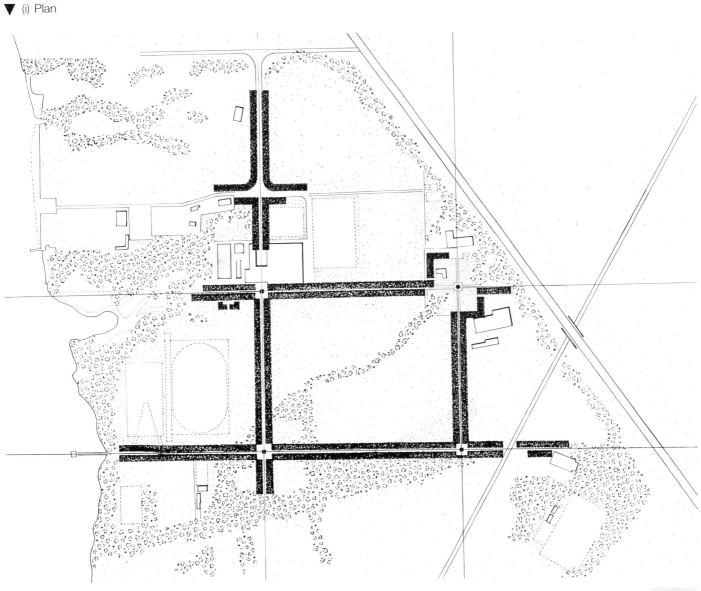

▲ (ii) View showing the relationship between the building structure, the structured landscape and the 'borrowed landscape' of the mountains

2.11 Quarry Park 'Motto Grande', Camorino, Switzerland

Paolo L. Bürgi

The site was provided by the removal of a portion of glacial moraine from the mountainside above the village of Camorino in the Magadino Plain, for the building of a road, leaving a plateau of about 1 ha of open land surrounded by forest. In this area trees were planted to designate spaces for particular purposes. The circular group of poplars in the centre, for community functions, has gaps to permit views of the mountains and towards a historical building in the village. In addition the path leading from it is designed to take advantage of the views of the surroundings. The drainage system of streams and naturalistic pools, is carefully considered to require minimal intervention – this includes a narrow water channel and spout producing a miniature water-fall. the inspiration for the design is illustrated by a drawing of Hokusai, reminding us that man has always intervened in the landscape, modifying it and interpreting the signs.

Figure 2.11 Quarry Park 'Motto Grande'

▲

(i) View from above

◀ (ii) Detail of wooden water channel with spout

49

◀ (iii) General view showing tree circle and mountains

◀ (iv) View of wild area

2.12 'A green spiral', Ticino, Camorino, Switzerland 1985

Paolo L. Bürgi

The aim was to stir emotions and to provoke intellectual reactions in visitors to this small square between the buildings of a Biochemical company in Ticino, Camorino, on the Magadino Plain of southern Switzerland, completed in 1985. The grassed area of 1500 m² has been planted with 100 Lombardy poplars arranged in a spiral marked by a line of uncut grass. The path between them, 4 m wide and 180 m long, begins with round stepping stones and terminates in a circular paved area with a sphere at the centre.

This is an unusual example of a design in which the expressive force is communicated entirely through living material, symbolizing both time and space, in a dynamic form reflecting rational values.

Figure 2.12 'A green spiral'
▼ (i) Aerial view

◀ (ii) View with building towards mountains

◀ (iii) Internal view

2.13 Stockley Park, Hillingdon, London, UK

Arup Associates
Landscape: Ede Griffiths Partnership and Charles Funke

Stockley Park is an international business park situated three miles north of London (Heathrow) Airport in Hillingdon; it represents an important partnership in development for both private and public use. It was created by transforming old gravel workings and a rubbish tip into 100 ha of parkland, with lakes, a golf course, playing fields and 35 ha devoted to business. The master plan by Arup Associates was prepared after extensive market research and detailed site analysis, and the implementation required the services of a Dutch reclamation specialist, who has been credited with designing the topsoil. The decision not to build the business park on landfill resulted in the transference of rubbish from the south to the north of the site where it had to be shaped into contours at 0.5 m intervals before capping: a total of about 6 million m³ of material was moved. The landscape is designed with two valleys linking the golf course to the north with the Grand Union Canal to the south, and all buildings are planned with access and views towards them and the lakes which they contain. In these areas the planting is relatively lush, with open park landscape in the areas between. There are three zones: the 'naturalistic' landscape of the golf course and the valleys, the 'geometric' forms of the district park and playing fields, and the contrasting linear and cellular forms of the business park that respond to the needs of the buildings and parking. The business park is formally planted with semi-mature species including lime trees, planes and hornbeams, while the valleys are informally planted with willows and other water-related species. Evergreen hedges screen service areas and define pathways, together with extensive shrub and ground-cover planting.

Stockley Park is a rare British example of a new landscape that is entirely man-made; in spite of the enormous cost it will provide a useful standard for the reclamation of all the other polluted wastelands of which we are the inheritors.

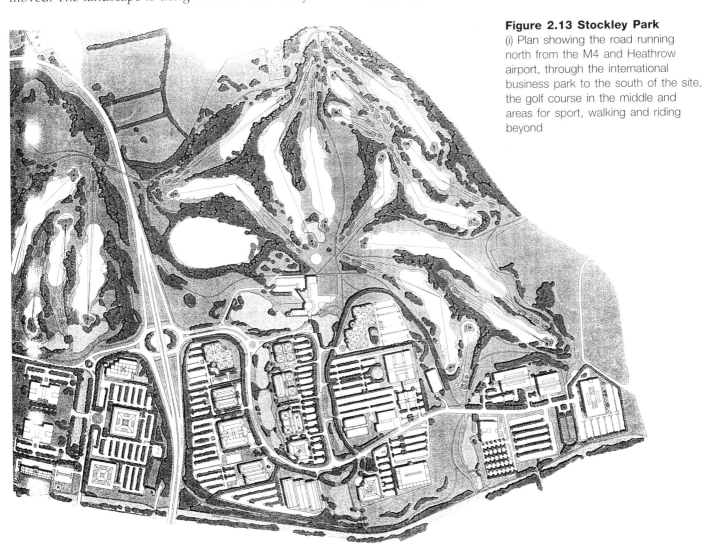

Figure 2.13 Stockley Park
(i) Plan showing the road running north from the M4 and Heathrow airport, through the international business park to the south of the site, the golf course in the middle and areas for sport, walking and riding beyond

(ii) View towards Arena social
building in the business park

(iii) View of offices across the lake

2.14 Gateway One, Basingstoke, UK 1976

Arup Associates: Architects, Engineers and Quantity
Surveyors

Figure 2.14 Gateway One

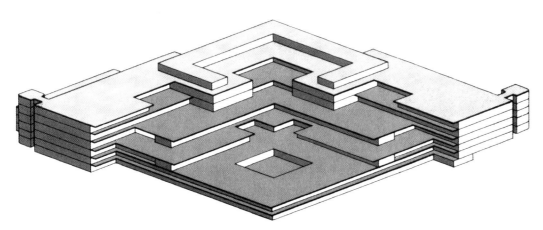

◀ (i) Isometric drawing

The development comprises new offices for Wiggins
Teape, the paper manufacturing firm, which was
moving from central London to the 'expanded town'
Basingstoke. Two broad aims guided the evolution of
the design: the need for a building based 'on a repeti-
tive module that would suit a variety of office activities,
and consideration for the staff in providing landscape
surroundings which would take full advantage of the
south-facing sloping site.' Each floor steps back from the
one below, providing roof terraces with gardens of two
kinds. The smaller, more intimate spaces are intensively
planted – which has given rise to the local description
'hanging gardens' – in contrast to larger areas adjoining
some of the communal rooms, which are more open
with lawns and shrub borders. The maintenance is facilitated by the avoidance of painted surfaces on the
buildings.

◀ (ii) Path outside offices with 'exotic' planting

◄ (iii) The luxuriance of the hanging gardens

2.15 NMB Bank, Amsterdam, The Netherlands

Jørn Copijn
Peter Rawstorne

The design for new office buildings was developed gradually from sketch designs produced by the architectural practice Alberts and Van Hut with the landscape architects Copijn Utrecht Groenadviseurs, between 1981 and 1988, when implementation was complete. It comprises 50 000 m² of office area for some 2400 employees, with underground services and car parking, located in the Bijlmeer Centre in southeast Amsterdam.

The aim was to produce a sense of place with which people could identify and in which they could feel 'at home' and in touch with nature. Accordingly, the scale of the building was broken down in plan to provide ten towers connected by an internal street, each having its own identity. The loose informal layout divides the site into a series of courtyards, each of which has been given its own character. Apart from a few areas around the edge, all of these are roof gardens placed over the car parks, designed to take a load of 800 kg per m² which permits a reasonable depth of soil without artificial substitutes. The planting – inspired by alpine ecology – is, however, carefully irrigated. There are three different themes: English, Japanese and Finnish. The English garden is characterized by a large cascade running down to a pond; and on the other side of the Public Relations Office to which it relates, there is a formal knot garden with ground cover and hedges. The Japanese garden is dominated by an irregular channel with stone patterns extending for a total length of 250 m, with vegetation including bamboo, Japanese maples and anemones, and primroses. The Finnish garden, by contrast, is based upon simple natural effects with plants growing on peat. These incude undulating clipped hedges and heather, and a large herb garden to serve the adjoining kitchen.

Figure 2.15 NMB Bank

◀ (i) General view towards buildings

◀ (ii) Waterfall in the Japanese garden

▼ (iii) Part plan

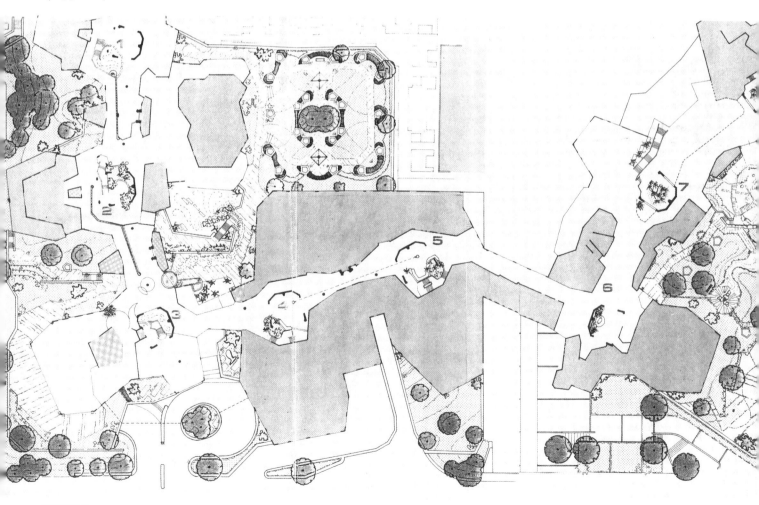

CHAPTER 3

Landscape and the city

Like a piece of architecture, the city is a construction in space, but one of vast scale, a thing perceived only in the course of long spans of time...
(Kevin Lynch, *The Image of the City*]

Awareness of space goes beyond cerebral activity. It engages the full range of senses and feelings, requiring the involvement of the whole self...
(Edmund Bacon, *Design of Cities*]

The city is defined by form and space. We experience it through channels of movement of various kinds: paths, roads, avenues, boulevards, streets, squares, gardens and parks – all enclosed or punctuated by buildings. Each has its own character and atmosphere, and its own uses, which might be regular or occasional, active or passive, spontaneous or regulated. These are not simple, nor are they random. Some have been planned as grand gestures of authority; some as recreational spaces to avoid social unrest; and many grow out of local decisions arising from long periods of human occupation. Some are artificial; some are natural.

Space flows naturally into cities with rivers, which act as valleys – conduits carrying clean and foul air, fresh water and sewage, and wildlife. Also, however cherished or abused they are, they act as *spatial* corridors offering long views and more or less continuous elevations of the opposite banks, which in many cases have been built up as promenades. Often they are complemented by the spatial geometry of the Renaissance, derived from the axial planning of the Romans. Although used, particularly in France, to express the power and authority of the state and the subjugation of nature, this was accompanied during the Baroque period, by a new conception of space: the capacity to organize it,

make it continuous, reduce it to measure and order, and to extend the limits of magnitude, embracing the extremely distant and the extremely minute: finally, to associate space with motion and time (Mumford, 1966).

This 'idealogy of power' as Mumford describes it, has given spatial structure and focus to most of our capital cities. It is seen at its most ambitious in Rome, its most dramatic in Paris and its most domestic in London.

Space was the medium used by Sixtus V on his appointment as Pope in 1586, to express the power of the Christian church in the city of Rome. He linked churches and other strategic points, marked by Egyptian obelisks (of which the city had a collection), with 'shafts of space' which determined the planning structure of Rome for generations after his death (Bacon, 1967). In Paris, Italian ideas of planning were adopted in stages from 1600, which determined the remarkable western expansion from the central area of the Bastille and the Louvre into the countryside. They formed the basis of the open-space planning of boulevards, squares and *rond points* by Haussmann for Napoleon III in the 1850s; also the recent Renaissance of the French park.

The city fathers in London had lacked both the vision and the sense of purpose to adopt Sir Christopher Wren's master plan for modernization of the West End after the fire: perhaps they were still smarting over his substitution of a Baroque St Paul's for the old Gothic cathedral. He did, however, succeed in creating two remarkable spatial complexes: Chelsea Hospital (1692), which links the King's Road, Chelsea, to the river by means of a series of squares; and the Royal Naval College at Greenwich (from 1699). The buildings of the riverside college are split to give precedence to the Queen's House by Inigo Jones (1629–40) seen against a backdrop of Greenwich Park with the asymmetrically placed Observatory, projecting a 'shaft of space' northwards for three km across the Isle of Dogs to a church, since disrupted by the unsympathetic commercial planning and oversized tower of Canary Wharf. More typically English are the forms of square, circus and crescent adapted for domestic use by landlords and developers during the eighteenth and nineteenth centuries in many towns and cities, combining enclosed private spaces, 'borrowed' landscape views, and changing axes to accommodate movement. All are combined in John Nash's sequence of parks and streets extending from Regent's Park to Buckingham Palace (from 1814).

Parks for the People

Public 'Promenades' became increasingly common from the eighteenth century, and after the French Revolution in 1789 these were supplemented by parks that had formerly been private. The idea of a peoples' park – a *Volksgarten* in which all social classes could mingle for the enjoyment of nature, informed and inspired by 'buildings with interesting pictures for the history of the nation, statues of their dead heroes and monuments to important events' – was developed by C.C.L. Hirschfeld (1742–92). It was influential in the design of the Englischer Garten in Munich by Sckell (from 1804), and more positively in the work of Peter Josef Lenné, who proposed both a Volksgarten and a national monument in remembrance of the war against Napoleon, in the Berlin Tiergarten (1819). J.C. Loudon (1783–1843) promoted the idea in England, commenting that parks should be designed 'less to display beautiful scenery than to afford a free wholesome air, and an ample uninterrupted promenade' – a significant departure from the Picturesque that had influenced him at the beginning of his career. By the end of the decade he was proposing public gardens to 'raise the intellectual character of the lowest classes of society'. In 1840 he completed Derby Arboretum, a small but highly innovative design for a city centre park. Three years later Joseph Paxton (1803–65) created the first major public park in England, at Birkenhead, across the river Mersey from Liverpool.

Paxton transformed the lower part of a dull site into a romantic landscape with lakes, hills and exotic trees; the upper part included areas for archery and cricket. The innovative circulation system comprised boundary roads for town traffic, a restricted central road and a carriage drive for pleasure traffic only. The meandering footpaths were carefully aligned to benefit from a contrived series of changing views. By 1851 the population of British cities exceeded that of the countryside.

With the rapid growth of industrial societies, parks such as that at Birkenhead, became a social and political necessity everywhere. They could never keep up with the demand. Although many started well, changing populations and changing fashions caused erosion of the original layouts, which were rarely redesigned (Goode, 1986).

The impetus for a new design approach came from Holland and from Sweden. Three large urban parks were created in Holland in the years following the First World War: Zuiderpark in the Hague (1920), the Kralinge Bos in Rotterdam (1927), and the Amsterdam Bosplan (1930). The last and most famous was a functional version of the fashionable romantic style by Cornelius van Eesteren and Jacoba Mulder. The character is derived directly from the reclaimed landscape with drainage ditches, canals and lakes, dividing areas devoted to all kinds of sports and recreation, including nature reserves. The natural assets of the site were also regarded as an important starting point in Sweden by Rutger Sernander (1866–1944) the Professor of Botany at Uppsala University, who argued against the artificiality of public parks. In spite of considerable opposition from the powerful parks departments, the idea was adopted into the policy of the Stockholm Parks Department, under its director (1936–38), Oswald Almqvist. As an architect he understood well the importance both of strategic planning and design policy; moreover, he was in touch with the most successful modern design movement in Europe. The result was a series of parks with integrated buildings, using hardy plants and emphasizing the character of the Swedish landscape. They provided models for the new towns and post-war developments of Europe (Andersson, 1993).

The motor vehicle has dominated post-war developments, prompting various methods of segregation. In the new towns these took the form of separate cycle and pedestrian systems, which tend to be little used. In the older towns and cities, pedestrian precincts or areas have become fashionable after much initial resistance, but they are often isolated. The ideal is to provide unifield systems in which housing, parks, gardens, play areas, shopping streets and public squares are all linked to one another and to the transport systems, but segregated from the dangers and pollution of traffic. Bacon refers to Simultaneous Movement Systems, using a drawing by Paul Klee to illustrate the multi-level complexity. The fact that these systems are often dealt with separately is counter-productive. Similarly, it is absurd to deal with them by giving priority to only one transport system, such as that of the motor vehicle, without providing viable alternatives. There are, however, encouraging signs, from many European countries that effective consideration is beginning to be given to all in the attempt to restore the city to the people.

3.1 The CIS (formerly the USSR)

The immediate post-war years were marked by a great enthusiasm for gardening and 'garden art' at all levels, beginning with fruit and vegetable gardens in the villages – an important means of livelihood – and flower gardens 'for the soul'. At the same time there was a national campaign for anti-erosion strip planting in the southern part of European Russia and the Ukraine, aimed at creating a new agricultural landscape. Unfortunately, the impetus was not sustained and some of the woodland belts were later cut down for firewood, although traces remain. Other long-term landscape planning projects included the replanting of woodlands for future industrial use, based on an idea formulated before the war, and the making of artificial lakes for water supply. These also suffered from changing priorities and consequent neglect.

In the cities there was great enthusiasm for more and better green spaces. People seemed to feel that good parks and gardens compensated for the problems of housing, and the Municipal authorities were able to involve all citizens. Those who were children during the 1950s and 1960s were directly involved in the spring-time 'Plant-a-Tree' campaign which has resulted in the well-wooded parks and spaces between blocks of flats in the larger cities. One of these was the Druzhba ('Friendship') Park sited in an old quarry to the north-west of Moscow. Others, such as the Nikitski Park, were based on existing woodlands.

This, and the Luzniki Park, established on reclaimed land, form part of the 'Green Wedge' master plan developed in the 1950s, which ensured that Moscow, like London and Berlin, has over 20 per cent of green open space, in spite of some erosion. The green wedge includes the gardens and planted avenues associated with the new high-rise buildings of Moscow State University which opened in 1953, extending over the river to the Luzniki Sports Park where the main city stadium was situated. The reclamation here has been successful and the trees have flourished, although the park has become cluttered with the addition of playing fields and snack bars. Also the botanic garden and the flower parterres associated with the university have recently suffered from neglect. The grounds of the All-Union Exhibition (VDNK) in northern Moscow opened in 1952, with pavilions and gardens representing the different republics, and has been turned over to commercial use since 1991.

The strong landscape tradition of Leningrad was expressed during the same period, in the restoration of historic parks and gardens, such as Peterhof and Puskin, and the creation of new ones. These included the Park of Culture and Rest that was conceived before the war,

(a)

(b)

Figure 3.1 The CIS

(i) Ekaterinburg (formerly Svedlovsk), Ural Mountains (a) square; (b) industrial 'sculpture' court

◀ (ii) Druzhba Park, Moscow; view over skating lakes towards housing blocks

(a)

(b)

▲ (iii) Sokolniki Park, Moscow (a) informal area with new pond and carved wood sculpture; (b) the Beaux Arts tradition is continued with the new plaza and fountain

but was made as a memorial to the siege of Piskariev; and Victory Park on the Moscow Prospect, containing lakes on the site of a quarry, with trees planted by the citizens.

Around 1960, green spaces, which are now flourishing, were created in many cities, including Penza, Orel and Omsk. There followed the concept of 'water-and-green', which was realized on a grand scale in Kiev in the Ukraine, bordering the wide Dnieper river. The same principle was followed in the 1980s in two projects, in the Crimea and the Ukraine, and in the Minsk river system. The first comprised the establishment of a series of small gardens linked by footpaths, along the banks of a fast-flowing stream in the Salgirka Valley, Simferopol; the second, a system of parks and gardens on freshly reclaimed riverside land. The river itself was the subject of reclamation and water purification measures, recently extended to include a second stream within the area of the city.

Although interest has been sustained in imaginative projects through competition, such as that for Detski Theme Park, little has been implemented, and maintenance standards have declined. This decline is balanced by an increasing interest in the cleansing of rivers and streams, reclaiming land in 'water-and-green' schemes, and conserving woodlands.

3.2 Denmark

During the 1950s the scope of work for landscape designers increased dramatically in the field of public (state) housing. Initially this was focused on the provision of small semi-private parks, but as the scale increased, due to the development of industrial building techniques, there was a need to create bolder, more open landscapes. The change was accompanied by a number of technical problems. The use of heavy machinery caused compaction of the ground, resulting in poor drainage and poor growing conditions. Increased public use (and abuse) also caused problems, and there were inevitable demands for more parking space.

The variety of work increased dramatically during the

Figure 3.2 Denmark

◀ (i) Trongaard Primary School, Lyngby (design: J.P. Schmidt, 1961). One of several types of public building that were regarded as prestige projects during the building boom of the 1960s. This building enclosed a number of 'exotic' courtyards containing water, granite paving and lush vegetation, in contrast to the more hard-wearing external areas. (a) One of the internal courtyards;

▼ (b) plan of the site

1960s, to include public and community facilities for the expanding suburbs and new towns. These included creches, schools, libraries and meeting halls, as well as some major building complexes such as hospitals and teaching institutions. The competition system began to offer opportunities for little-known designers; particularly for expanding churchyards and the creation of new cemeteries. In the 1970s, new universities were established in Alborg and Roskilde, and the Technical College moved out of the centre of Copenhagen to a new campus. In recognition of the changing nature of the work, the title 'garden architect' was changed in 1969 to 'landscape architect'.

Patterns of housing and settlement changed again in the 1970s and 1980s. Low-density housing again became popular, with greater stress upon human scale and attempts to recover the traditional ambience of old towns and villages. Rehabilitation and the improvement of city centres became fashionable, giving way in the present decade, to an increasing tendency towards

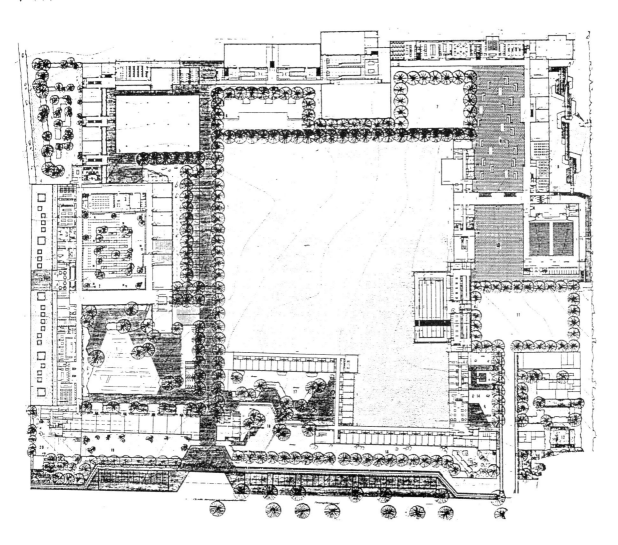

monumentalism in dense urban structures. Landscape planning has developed as a discipline, with the need for large-scale design for a new motorway system.

The strong Japanese influence of the 1950s was succeeded, in the 1960s, by a large-scale simplicity, accompanied by highly detailed private spaces. This process continued in the next two decades, with a greater interest in the variety both of houses and public spaces, reflecting an increasing environmental awareness and a weakening of the traditional influence of the parks authorities.

▲ (ii) Refugiet at Logumkloster (design: J.P. Junggreen Have, 1961). The designer has sought to express an atmosphere of timelessness and tranquility in the courtyard of this modern monastery, by the use of static forms of clipped beech and yew. (a) Courtyard

(b) plan of the site ▶

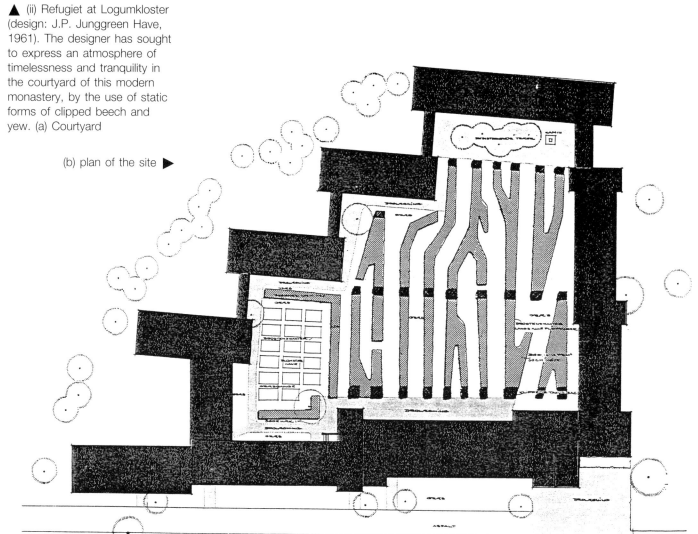

(iii) Housing at Sjolund, Hellebaek (design: Svend Kirkegaard, 1978). The 1970s were marked by the return of low-density housing with layouts ranging from the strictly geometric to the informal based on old villages. Respect for the landscape hierarchy of scales and land uses from the intimate spaces close to the buildings, which are grouped beside a small lake, to the wooded surroundings. Parking is limited to the perimeter of the site.

▲ (a) The intimate spaces between the houses are defined by black timber walls planted with ivy

▲ (c) houses are clustered around a small lake in the grounds of a former estate

▼ (b) plan of the site

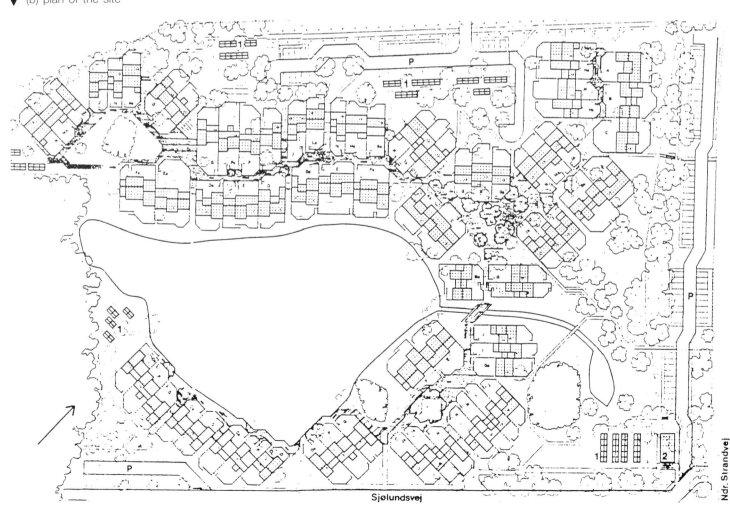

3.3 Park system of Milton Keynes, UK

Peter Youngman: Landscape Planner
Neil Higson: Landscape Architect
Milton Keynes Development Corporation

The linear parks system is based on the three river valleys which cross the designated area of the new city. As virtually all the land falls within the flood plain it provided a logical basis for parkland, albeit of various types, from active sports to passive recreation and agricultural grazing. The concept was that of the character of English National Parks, although much smaller in scale – an expression of *rus in urbe* in the relationship to the city. The large area (about 1800 ha) demanded careful strategies both for management and the activities, which are linked by footpaths, bridleways and cycle tracks. Ancient sites and historic monuments have been included in the system, with improved access and viewing facilities. The system network is described by the analogy of a string of beads: the string represents

the routes; the beads of varying sizes and degrees of attraction represent the car parks, picnic areas, cafes, gardens, sculpture and historic sites. The 'strings' are colour-coded, including greenways, redways (cycle-paths) and local leisure route paths surfaced with buff-coloured or yellowish local gravel. All are seen against a background setting of woodland and pasture, forest and water, interspersed with commercial recreation sites.

The Ouzel Valley Linear Park

Although narrow, the river Ouzel was inclined to flood the broad valley, and flood protection measures had to be taken. These included the formation of a series of balancing lakes with varying water levels, including Willen in the north and Caldecotte in the south, with a small lake in the middle. In addition to the small river Ouzel, the Grand Union Canal passes through the valley, following the contours of the western side. This is distinguished by regular planting of Lombardy

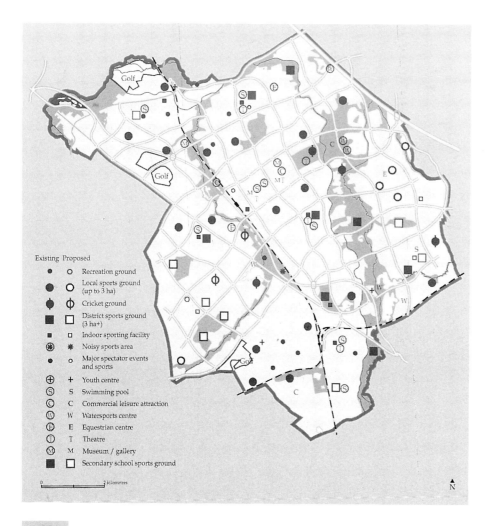

Figure 3.3 Park system of Milton Keynes

◀ (i) Plan of the city (design: MKDC) showing parks and open spaces; the Ouzel valley with the balancing lakes running along the east side

(ii) Lombardy poplars have been planted along the Grand Union Canal to emphasize its man-made character; this 'leisure route', bridle path and tow path defines the western edge of the valley path

(iii) Lakeside pub and watersports centre from informal parkland area in Ouzel Valley

▲ (iv) Woodlands of small trees (Field maple) have been planted to give the illusion of distance; view east from lookout hill in Campbell Park

Poplars – emphasizing its man-made character as it cuts through the city – and it is linked with the main body of the park.

Caldecotte Lake provides a setting for housing, business and recreation, including boating and sailing. Walton Lake, in the middle of the park – originally used for balancing before the completion of the other lakes – has been devoted to nature conservation, an appropriate function close to the medieval church and eighteenth century manor house, Walton Hall, headquarters of the Open University (see below). It is a lake filled with islands, planted with reeds and varieties of species of willow, which has become a sanctuary for wildlife.

Willen Lake, at the northern end of the valley park, is divided by a spillway separating the northern half, which is designated as an environment for bird nesting and feeding, and the southern half which is recreational. The western shore forms a popular family and visitor park with hotel, cafes, and areas for water-sports, picnics and children's play.

In addition to its important links with the business and educational institutions of the present and future, the linear park serves both to emphasize the structure of the city and to conserve its roots in groups of old buildings and the historical nuclei of villages lining the valley.

The Villages Grid Square: Great Linford

Michael Lancaster: Landscape Consultant

Great Linford was a linear village of typically mixed cottages adjoining Linford Hall, a spectacular stone manor house of the seventeenth century with a pair of outlying pavilions, a round pond and vestiges of a formal garden. The village itself was designated as a Conservation Area, but the surrounding fields provided sites for new housing by a number of different architects. The landscape design for these ranges from the small- to the large-scale and from the formal to the informal; one of the most successful covering a string of argricultural drainage ponds linked to that of the manor house. In an attempt to echo the English vernacular, the architect, Martin Richardson, chose to cluster the houses' terraces tightly around a central car park, freeing the landscape around. Although underground drainage dried up most of the agricultural ponds, one was saved (largely because of the agreed surveillance of the adjoining house-owner) and the meandering line of the agricultural ditch planted with willows. This acts as a focus for the site, modulating the light, and, at the same time, consolidating the important links with the past (see Natural colour section).

The Open University: Walton Hall, Milton Keynes

Michael Lancaster: Landscape Consultant

The eighteenth-century manor house situated on a low mound with a walled garden and medieval church, surrounded by a park with ancient trees, seemed an ideal site for the new concept, a 'university of the air'. The staff numbers were originally small, requiring a car park for only 100 cars, which was concealed by a steep grass mound. The geometry of this served the additional function of an indicator, directing the eye beside the avenue planted with Horse Chestnuts towards the principal offices in the old Manor House. New buildings enclosed courtyards, one simply of grass around an old cedar tree; another with an informal parterre replacing an old herb garden.

(v) Open University, Walton Hall (design: Michael Lancaster, landscape architect; Fry, Drew and Partners, architects).

▲ (a) The first car park adjoining the old church is concealed behind a geometric grass-covered mound which extends to the entrance of Walton Hall

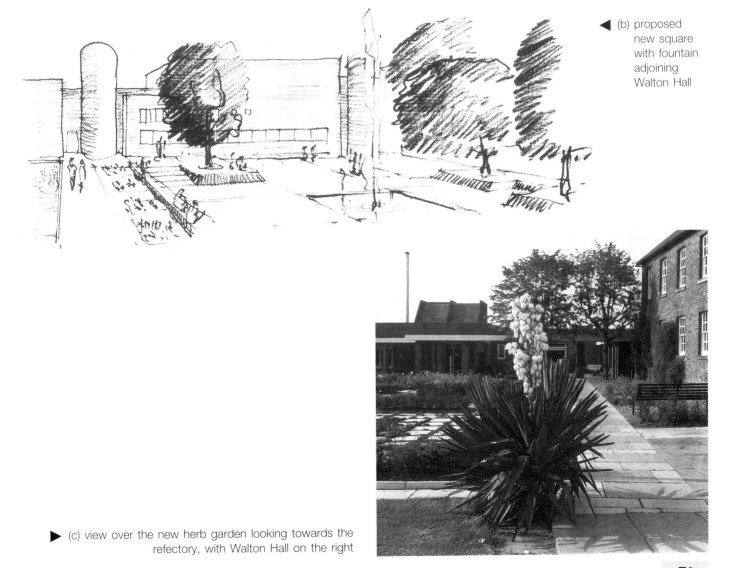

◄ (b) proposed new square with fountain adjoining Walton Hall

▶ (c) view over the new herb garden looking towards the refectory, with Walton Hall on the right

3.4 Leybourne Park, Hawley Road, Camden, London, UK 1974–6

Michael Lancaster

The design problem was to provide durable active and passive recreation areas on a site bisected by the arches of the railway and situated on a continuous pedestrian route between Hampstead and the West End of London. The geometric form was determined on one hand by the shape of the 'kickabout' areas on one side of the arches and the decision to provide a 'square' to relate to the terrace of houses in neighbouring Leybourne Close, which were being rebuilt. It was considered desirable that both areas should be visible from the outside except on the edges where screening from the busy roads was important. This was achieved by means of raised brick beds with dense shrub planting and London Plane trees.

The areas in between were similarly divided by banks with battered brick walls, carefully arranged to provide a tapering vista towards the Victorian church, the only significant building on this part of the site. Block walls enclosing seats immediately in front of the church are in stone colour to match the stone of the church, in contrast to the red brick of the battered brick walls.

When it was decided that two of the arches, which were originally open, should be filled in with a site office, the opportunity was taken to paint a simple *trompe l'oeil* pattern on them, adding colour to the play area. The formal sitting and walking area was paved with a special pattern of concrete slabs laid in gravel, with a raised grass area in the centre, to avoid too much erosion by walking. Unfortunately the area soon became unusable for small children because residents used it for their dogs and it has since been removed.

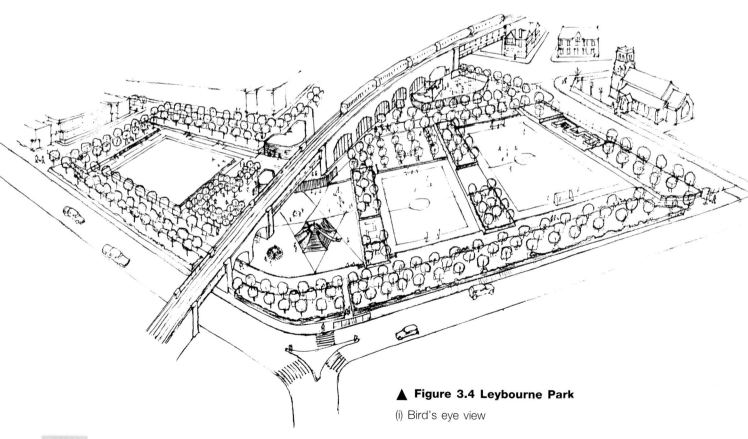

▲ **Figure 3.4 Leybourne Park**

(i) Bird's eye view

72

▲ (ii) The exaggerated perspective achieved by manipulating the levels and the flanking walls adds stature to the church. The stone of the church wall is echoed by the colour of the blocks surrounding the seats

◀ (iii) The formal passive area

3.5 Everton Park, Liverpool, UK 1967

Competition design by Michael Lancaster and
Derek Lovejoy Associates (First Prize)

The design was generated by the dynamic zig-zag line
of the old road running down the sloping ridge of the
site, from the cluster of old buildings, including the
church, library and public house. The intention was to
preserve the 'gritty' northern character of this area,
extending it with a rectangular boating lake, linked by
means of a stone-lined channel with water running
down alongside the old road, now converted to carry a
tram, to a lower set of pools in the modern idiom, with
light tower, disco area, restaurant, café and bar.
The intention of the design was to forge a link between
the old and the new: the remnants of late nineteenth-
century working class Liverpool in the cluster of public
buildings at the top end of the site, the great concrete
slab blocks overshadowing the western edge (since
demolished), and the surrounding red brick streets.

Figure 3.5 Everton Park

▼ (i) Plan

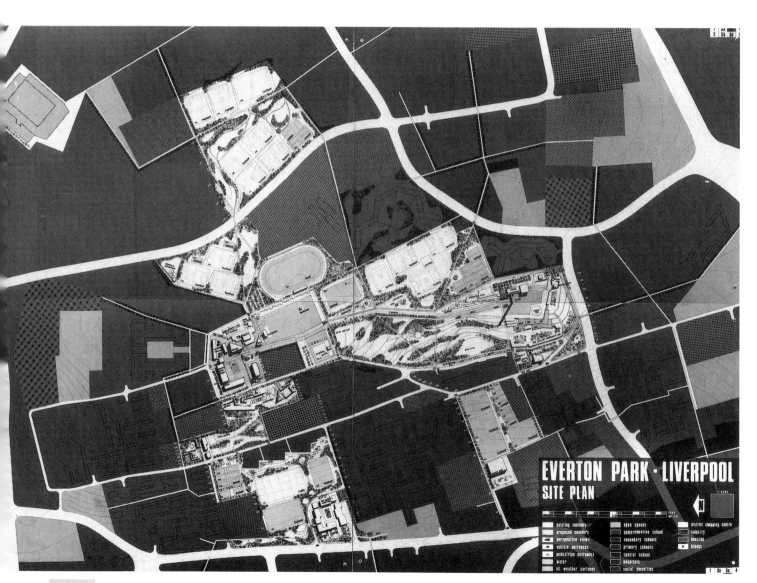

▲ (ii) A new rectangular boating pool was proposed at the top end of the site to emphasize and unify the buildings – church, library and public house – representing the old Liverpool. This was linked to the new area by an old tramway and a deep stone-lined channel with water running down the slope of the ridge to the pool at the bottom

▲ (iii) The lower area was seen as a land and cityscape of the future, with fountains, pools, a light tower and discos – fitting for the city that gave birth to the Beatles

3.6 The Renaissance of the French park

In 1977 a directly elected city government was established in Paris, which had been governed by a prefect since the commune of 1871. Control of the area between the Peripherique and the two large parks to the east and the west – the Bois de Vincennes (995 ha) and the Bois de Boulogne (825 ha) became the responsibility of the Mayor (Jacques Chirac) and his right-wing RPR party. Since their election some 102 *espaces verts* – parks, gardens and squares – have been created as elements within a master plan covering all environmental aspects of the city. The example has been followed by other cities.

Innovation in design began to appear towards the end of the 1960s, notably in the work of Jacques Simon (b.1929). In Le Zac de Chatillons (1968) a small park (40 ha) in Reims, he experimented with sensuously curved mounding and informal planting to contrast with the strongly rectangular forms of buildings. This was followed in 1970 by Le Parc St John Perse (18 ha) in the same city, in which he defines large open areas of playing fields with planted earth mounds. The park blends the softly curving open fields with dense thickets which heighten the contrast and define clear spatial boundaries. Here, Simon sculpts and expresses his feeling for the land.

Simon's influence can be seen in the contrasting use of textures and voluptuous land form employed by Michel Courajoud (b.1937) in *Le Parc de Coudrays*, Yvelines (*c*. 1975). The landscape becomes almost like a succession of green waves where children can hide, dream and play'. By using a wide variety of geometric and organic forms, Courajoud has succeeded in transforming a dull flat suburban area to one that is rich in experience.

Figure 3.6 Renaissance of the French park

(i) Le Parc de Coudrays (design: Michael Courajoud)

◀ (a) general view

◀ (b) Grass-covered mounds
    alternating with shrubby
    willows

◀ (c) formal area

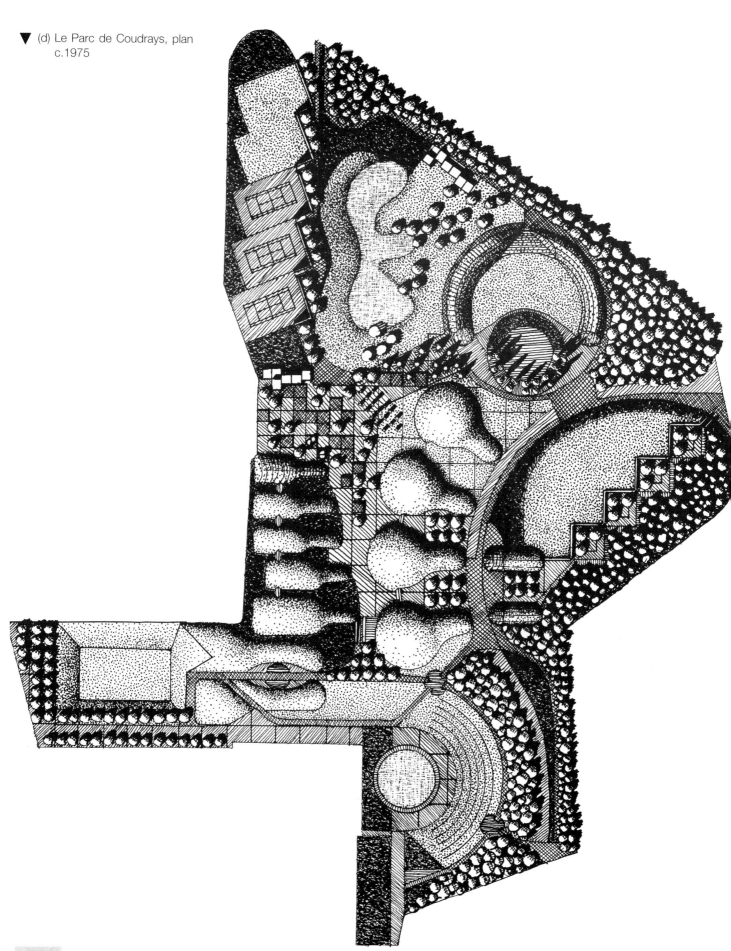

Le Parc du Sausset, begun in the early 1980s, marks a major shift in scale for French landscape design; also for the designers, Michel Courajoud, Edith Girard, Claire Courajoud and Jacques Coulon. The 290 ha (700 acre) park situated in a working class area to the north of Paris is being constructed in phases with a projected completion date in the middle of the next century. The formal axiality of the layout is a reflection of French tradition, but the subtle articulation between the masses of trees and the lawn areas is reminiscent of Simon's park in Rheims.

▲ (ii) Le Parc de Sausset (design: Michael Courajoud, Edith Giraud, Claire Courajoud and Jacques Coulon). (a) tree planting

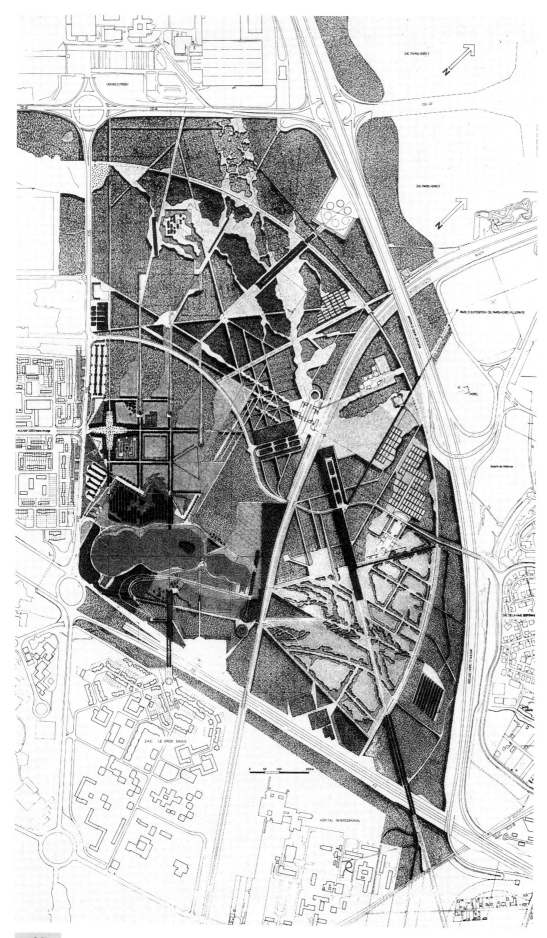

◀ (b) plan

Le Parc de la Villette is distinguished in terms of landscape design by the work of Alexandre Chemetoff (b.1950) and Martine Renan (b.1958), in *Le Jardin des Bambous* (1988). The bold and intricate geometry of the built elements in this sunken garden provide a perfect foil for the rich exotic qualities of the bamboo, emphasizing the idea of wilderness: 'a masterpiece which achieves sensuousness with a perfect blend of Cartesian rigour'. Similar contrasts of colour and texture have been employed by Chemetoff in *Les Jardins Schlumberger* (completed 1986) in Bagneux to the south of Paris. The contrasts between the building – offices refurbished by Renzo Piano – water, paths and planting are all emphasized to give a sense of controlled intimacy to the garden, a place to be seen rather than used. An unusual variation on the theme of landscape architecture, is Chemetoff's project using blue-painted poles and tree-planting along an 18 km stretch of the Toulouse motorway, as part of an ambitious scheme aimed at integrating new infrastructures into the existing landscape.

◀ (iv) Le Parc André Citroen (design: Gilles Clement and Alain Provost). (a) View towards the central area

▼ (b) path in one of the enclosed gardens

Le Parc André Citroën is part of a large development including offices on the site of the old Citroën works to the south-west of Paris; the subject of a competition for which the joint winners, Gilles Clement and Alain Provost, were commissioned. It is based upon a formal French plan, but scaled down, and includes many unusual features. Gilles Clement, who has been accustomed to working on private gardens, proposes a '*friche urbaine*' – a fallow area in which people can learn about nature; and there are many enclosed gardens on different themes bordering the formal rectangle in the centre which is surrounded by water features. The park will eventually be opened up to the Seine.

Typical of the medium-sized parks in the new towns surrounding Paris, is *La Base de Loisirs de Ognes/Le Parc du Mandinet*, Val de Marne (1989), by Gilles Vexlard. It shows a distinct correlation between the surrounding built form and plant massing. The landscape comprises bands of plants of varying height, conceived as a part of a fairly rigid geometric system of spatial organization. Vexlard is also the designer of *La Treille*, one of the theme gardens in Le Parc de la Villette. This comprises a high metal pergola for vines, rising from paved terraces with running water: an example of the constructed 'hard' architectural approach to landscape design, further examples of which can be seen in the work of Jacques Coulon.

The Brutalist trend is exemplified by the work of the architect Jacques Coulon in *Le Jardin de L'Ilot Gandon* (13th Arrondissement) a site dominated by massive residential towers. For his effects, he depends almost entirely upon built elements: paving patterns, sculptural elements, a *trompe l'oeil* seat with ceramic tiles, and a minimum of planting. On the sea-front promenade at St Valery en Cau, he relies entirely on patterned concrete, gravel and stone (1989).

▲ (vi) Sea front at St Valery en Cau (design: Jacques Coulon). View showing the relationship of the new patterned elements in various shades of pink and brown concrete with the breakwaters and shingle of the beach

A new generation of designers including G. Péré, M. Rascle, Denis Fontaine (Ilex), V. Lathiere and F. Carriere have combined to develop a new kind of park in the heavily built-up area surrounding Valenton in the Val-de-Marne. *Le Parc de la Plage Bleue* is based on an old lake formed by gravel extraction, which has been used for leisure purposes since 1979. The designers responsible for the overall design (Ilex), have succeeded in throwing off the chains of the formal French tradition, in favour of a strongly controlled geometry of curves, incorporating a number of mannerist ideas. The work is in four phases, spanning the years 1990–96; the first phase, as well as the master plan, is the responsibility of Ilex.*

*Text by Christophe Girot with additional material from Robert Holden, Sarah-Jenny Zarmati and Denis Fontaine (Ilex).

(vii) Parc de la Plage Bleue, Valenton (design, Ilex).
(a) plan

▼ (b) tree planting

▼ (c) view towards the lake

3.7 New Spanish parks

The political changes of the 1970s sparked off an era of social reform. In order to be elected, new parties were forced to face up to social problems, which had been exacerbated in the cities by excessive speculation and poor construction. The New Constitution of 1978 established a new planning vocabulary of open spaces, including: 'Green Belts', 'Green Zones', 'Landscape Areas', 'District and Peripheral Parks' (*Cinturion Verde, Zonas Verdes, Areas Ajardinadas, Parques de Barrio, Parques de Perificos*). The new guidelines and regulations encouraged specific developments for the rehabilitation of towns and cities, which were boosted by the establishment of National Town Planning Awards, which had the effect of enhancing property values. Also, the debate about public space stimulated neighbourhood groups to organize local competitions, such as the Madrid Gardens Competition of 1981, providing opportunities for young and little-known designers.

Larger-scale projects included the remodelling of the Turia riverbed passing through Valencia and the green corridor of the Manzanares River in Madrid. In addition, large numbers of urban and suburban open spaces have been created or renovated in many cities; particularly in Barcelona, which was further boosted by developments in preparation for the Olympic Games (1992).

Figure 3.7 New Spanish parks
▼ (i) El Peine de los Vientos, San Sebastian (design: Pena Ganchegui; sculptor: Eduardo Chillida). (a) Plan; (b) sea spray fountains

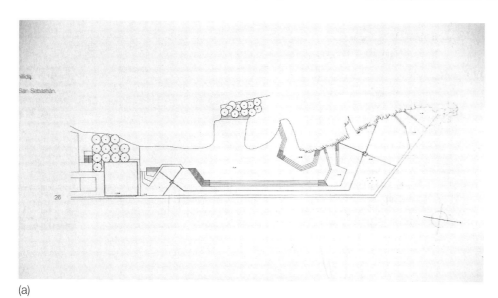

(a)

(b)

El Peine de los Vientos, San Sebastian (The comb of the winds)

Luis Pena Ganchegui: Architect
Eduardo Chillida: Sculptor

The site, comprising pink blocks of Porrino granite at the base of the sea cliffs on the edge of the city, dictated the design for a small park. According to Eduardo Chillida, 'This place is the origin of everything, the real creator of this work is itself. I have discovered it and pay tribute to it . . . a symbol of nature's encounter with the city.'

The sculpture represents an open pair of pliers which emerge from the rock and are cut away against the skyline. The park emphasizes the power of nature generally through the experience of changing weather in terms of the elements of sea and rock; and specifically in the hidden pipes that channel the power of the waves into spray fountains from the paved surface. These 'sonic' connections also produce miniature rainbows.

Pena Ganchegui is remarkable for his sensitivity to the context in which he works, in particular for his ability to capture to the full the experience of the landscape.

▼ (ii) Parque Olivar de la Hinojosa, Madrid (design: Emilio Esteras Martin, Jose Luis Esteban Penelas). (a) Plan; (b) view towards pyramidal hill

(a)

Parque Olivar de la Hinojosa, Madrid

This 220 hectare park, situated within the Park of the Nations complex, takes its name from the memorial olive tree. The park is designed on the principle of a large distributor ring, one kilometre in diameter, which is both functional and symbolic. Inside there are several gardens, including a rain garden, a sound garden and the Garden of Three Cultures. Outside, the planting is of larger scale, defining access squares and parking areas. The squares divide the crossing points of the ring into four different areas, representing the seasons. Water is a major feature: a 1.9 km long canal bisects the park and terminates in two pools, to the north and the south. The complex is deliberately artificial, with parabolic, arc and geyser fountains reaching up to 40 metres high. The park is dominated by three artificial mountains which provide important viewpoints. One is smooth and curved, covered with a grass lawn. Another has the form of a truncated pyramid, covered by different coloured shrubs. High level circulation is provided in certain areas by footbridges and ramps.

Within the park there is a conservatory devoted to tropical and sub-tropical plants, cactii and succulents. Tree planting comprises 76% deciduous and 24% coniferous species. Future extensions will include a golf course and an 8000-seat auditorium.

(b)

(a)

(b)

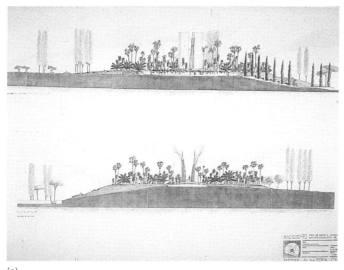

(c)

▲ (iii) Jardin de la Tres Culturas, Madrid (design: Myriam Silber Brodsky). (a). Plan; (b) symbolic ruins of the city wall in the Jewish Garden; (c) cross-section

Jardin de las Tres Culturas, Madrid

Myriam Sillber Brodsky

The garden represents the three cultures of Spain: Christian, Jewish and Islamic, turning around the common theme of Paradise. The three-hectare site occupies the northeast quadrant of the Parque del Olivar de la Hinojosa in the Campo de las Naciones area, to the northeast of Madrid. The garden, between the river and the olive grove, constitutes part of the European Capital Cultural programme for Madrid 1992.

The approach is from a small circular area in the olive grove, via a footbridge to the Garden of Paradise, situated on a larger, raised, circular platform, containing the Tree of Life sculpture, in concrete, steel and wood. From it there is access to each of the three gardens. Like the four rivers of the biblical Eden and the Koranic Paradise, four irrigation channels divide this space, which is planted with palm trees, representing an oasis.

The Claustro de las Cantigas (Christian garden) was named after the musical interest of King Alfonso the Learned, who created the famous Cantigas de Santa Maria. The garden, based upon a medieval example, is entered by a door with a bell, and the space is cruciform, containing four pools with a central platform for musical performances, the whole surrounded by a colonnade. Vegetation consists of apple trees, rosemary, lavender, laurel bushes and irises.

The Vergel de Granados (Jewish garden) was inspired by the Bible. Its name refers to one of the most poetic images, in the Cantar de los Cantares. The ideal city prophesied by Ezekiel overlooks a square comprising a grid of different textures in paving, coloured sands and plants, surrounded by the remnants of the city walls. The paved area is broken up by the outline of David's shield. Water flows from a fountain into channels beside the walls. The area is planted with pomegranates, cypress and olive trees, and waterside plants; the surrounding 'desert' is represented by rocks and palm trees.

The Estancia de las Delicias (the Islamic garden) is like an oriental carpet. From a pavilion raised in the centre of an eight-pointed star, paths and water-channels emanate between different levels of garden. Materials include bricks and tiles, and plants include palm trees, cypress, lilac, roses and jasmine, symbolic of Islam.

Mixed woods of Black Poplar, 'Paradise trees', and pine form the large circle of the Three Cultures Garden, until they become lost in the basic grid of the Parque del Olivar de la Hinojosa.

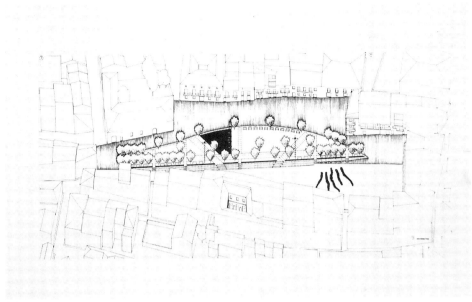

(a)

(b)

Plaza de la Corredera, Monbeltran, Avila

Juan Antonio Cortes, Maria Teresa Munoz: Architects

In 1984 the Direccion de Arquitectura del MOPU commissioned the Plaza, which was executed in 1987, by Castilla and Leon Board. It is the principal urban space of the town of Monbeltran, lying on the south-facing slopes of the Gredos Mountains, in the province of Avila. The area of 6 km² is long and irregular, a slope of 7 metres from top to bottom, and it is dominated by views of the mountains.

The designers' response to this irregular space was to introduce a new geometry that would provide a central focus, while allowing the edges to relate to the surroundings, and at the same time separating the traffic from the pedestrians. The geometric 'island' reveals the natural slope of the ground and expresses in its pattern, the lines of the roads entering the plaza. It is animated by fountains, pools and running water. The five irregular 'tongues' of water crossing the pedestrian area, symbolize the valley with its five villas. The trees (*Prunus pissardi nigra*) have been chosen for their small stature and their pink and bronze-red colour, to blend with the surroundings.

(a)

(b)

◀ (v) Plaza de la Corredera, Monbeltran (design: Juan Antonio Cortes and Maria Teresa Munoz). (a) View towards mountains; (b) the 'five tongues of water'

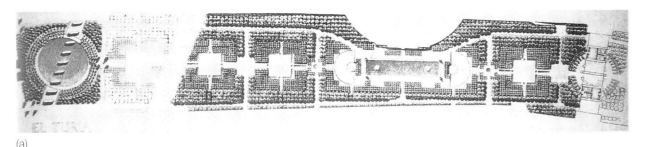

(a)

(b)

▲ (vi) El Jardin de Turia, Valencia
(design: Vetges i Mediterranea,
Ricardo Bofill Taller de
Arquitectura). (a) Plan; (b)
bridge area

El Jardin del Turia, Valencia

Vetges i Mediterranea
Ricardo Bofill, Taller de Arquitectura

As a result of the floods in 1957 the waters of the river Turia were diverted, and a motorway and the railway were included in the development plan (Plan General de 1966). In 1976 the plan was modified and the land given to the city for a public park.

The river passes through urban areas of the city, including historical, residential and industrial settlements. The intention was to create a green space that would transform the image of the city.

The Garden of Turia has been conceived as a sequence of geometric gardens arranged within a large pine wood (*Pinus pinea*), which follows the course of the river. Implementation has been phased, covering two sectors which are not continuous. Sector 2, Robella's Azud, of 120 475 m², has been designed by the team Vetges i Mediterranea.

Sector 10, which is not in sequence with Robella's Azud, has an area of 135 275 m², and was designed by the team Taller de Arquitectura. This contains a historical bridge and a new music auditorium.

The specific aim was to achieve unity between the different sectors and their surroundings along the length of the river valley, and to exploit the uses of water in different ways. According to Ignacio Veciana, 'Our concept of a public garden is based on a philosophy of natural balance between resources and design, to which is added the Roman conception of public space as a place for meeting, with different functions and hierarchies, using indigenous trees, including pines, cypresses, palms, oaks, orange and olive trees . . . .'

The Taller de Arquitectura group were influenced by the Islamic gardens of Ruzafa, particularly with reference to the music auditorium (Palacio de la Musica). Here the traditional Arab relationship between music and architecture is expressed: the two harmonies combining in a scene 'where rhythm is king'.

Barcelona

It is the nature of cities to re-create themselves or die. But usually the process is piecemeal, or at least inadequately coordinated with all the complex pressures for growth and development. As a trading city of the Phoenicians (founded 300 BC), which developed its own trading empire in the Middle Ages, Barcelona grew to be the major industrial city of Catalonia and the whole of Spain. Between 1818 and 1860 the population doubled, and poverty, pollution and disease were rife. The antidote was far-reaching. In 1866 the city was extended to include the villages of Gracia, Sarria and Sant Andreu i Horta, with a grid system which guaranteed basic standards of space, daylight and air to every citizen, and, most importantly, access to services and public transport (Woodward, 1992). Catalan *Modernisme* – the movement with which Gaudi was to become identified – dominated architecture. A further stimulus was provided by the International Exhibition of 1929 which included a bogus Spanish village as well as the German pavilion by Mies van der Rohe, regarded (somewhat later) as one of the seminal works of modern architecture.

The most recent opportunity for re-planning and development occurred at the end of the Fascist regime in 1975. As reported in *Domus*:

'No other metropolis has so cleverly utilized public space as a foundation for rethinking the concept of the city, thoroughly examining the related design and methodological issues. By treating it as the catalyst and the borderline of urban conflicts and social tensions, public space once again became a "heart" capable of regenerating morphological hierarchies and improving vast depressed urban areas.' (*Domus*, 1992.)

The resurgence of the city was initiated by the Mayor Pasquall Maragall, who commissioned Oriel Bohigas, Professor of Architecture in the University, to produce an urban policy in 1978. This included medium-scale designs that could be implemented in the medium term, and gave high priority to the questions of design choices, the new authority of space. The starting point was the realization that the idea of public space promoted by the Modern Movement had been a failure, and both the plaza and the street were re-addressed in an attempt to turn them into central factors in urban development. Dozens of projects were produced through collaboration between architects, artists and landscape architects. Some were experimental and too charged with abstract ideas, some were considered too architectural – inevitable in a situation dominated by architects – also, no less inevitably, some have been criticized by members of the small profession of landscape architects for their hardness – the limited use of plants and soft surfaces. Nevertheless, the comprehensive approach dealing with traffic, public transport and commercial demands, based upon the supremacy of the pedestrian, has established new standards of urban design. In the words of Maragall 'the city is a sign of identity, a testimony to the history of social and economic change, and a proof of cultural achievement.'

▲ (viii) Jardins de les Corts (design: Carme Fiol and Pascual Vidal) View from above

The policy originally conceived by Bohigas in 1978 aimed gradually to eliminate the dichotomy between the centre and the outskirts by multiplying the urban cores which were expected to generate their own development and increase property values. Older areas of the city were earmarked for 'sanitization' (restoration and conservation) – a policy which was later revised to one which may be described as 'creative conservation'. This included a pioneering colour plan for Barcelona (1986–91) based upon the principle of colour as an organizing medium rather than one used for merely decorative purposes. Beginning with such obvious areas as advertising and colour in new building applications, the project developed into specific areas, such as La Rambla, for which comprehensive colour proposals have been implemented under the direction of the architect Josep Hernandez-Cros. Although recognizing the significance of historical precedents, these proposals – unlike the majority of such schemes – are based upon the employment of colour as a unifying and co-ordinating medium.

Realization of the importance of the street and the plaza – which had been neglected by the Modern Movement – was a starting point in Bohiga's policy. Outlying districts were deliberately chosen for increased urbanization, with the park as 'a new monument'. In this way innumerable projects were developed as elements of the overall plan. But they had the advantage of individuality and experimentation, expressing the ideas of artists and professionals in response to local needs (*Domus* May 1992).

Local involvement was always paramount, Barcelona being a city 'where municipal elections are fought over park design issues – not whether to have parks' (Holden, 1988). For his 'urban interventions' Bohigas cites Camillo Sitte, Kevin Lynch, Aldo Rossi, and Leon Krier as advocates of the park and civic design to humanize the city.

The humanization process has been assisted by major engineering works to integrate the urban highways into the fabric of the city, the removal of old industries, and the reclamation of the waterfront for public use – the Moll de la Fusta. Technology has been used again, but creatively – not callously to destroy the city in improving communications – to facilitate its humanization. It is celebrated everywhere in civic spaces adorned with modern sculpture, and even with its own park, the Parc de l'Espana Industrial. This incorporates a grid of plane trees with both hard and soft areas, but it is dominated by concrete towers clad in granite and red and yellow tiles, with floodlights on top. It is a place for both daytime and night-time use.

A further boost to the development of the city came with preparations for the Olympic Games in 1992. This was concentrated on Montjuich, the hill to the west of the city where planning for the 1935 Olympics had taken place. Apart from the design work immediately associated with the games, the development included the creation of a Memorial Garden for the casualties of the Spanish Civil War, adjoining the huge municipal cemetery. This highly sensitive design by Beth Gali (landscape architect) is a refreshing link between the old and the new, between nature and technology. The entrance is by a wide ramp of grass-jointed granite slabs, with cypresses on one side. At the top there are stone columns on which are inscribed the names of the fallen. Beyond and inside the old quarry are a lawn and a reflecting pool with a wall of rocks, setting the mood.

Although there is talk of recovering 'green' space, it tends to be in abstract terms, in the manner of northern European town planning in the immediate post-war years. There is no suggestion of softening canalized river-beds where they pass through the city. The young and numerically weak landscape profession lacks the biological and ecological backup for such ambitious measures, or indeed for full participation in the 'hard' civic projects.

The great success of Barcelona is in the total acceptance of contemporary needs and values. For once the needs of the pedestrian and the inhabitant have been recognized, but they have not been recognized piecemeal; their acceptance derives from and relates to the needs of transport, commerce and industry. 'No other metropolis has so cleverly utilized public space as a foundation for re-thinking the concept of the city' (*Domus*, 1992).

La Plaza de la Estacion de Sants, Barcelona

Albert Viaplana, Helio Pinon, Ehric Miralles: Architects

The square was commissioned by the City of Barcelona, and completed in 1983. The architects chose a simple visual language of hard-wearing industrial materials as an appropriate expression for the renovation of the city, without reference to historical influences. The square is partly covered by a high canopy or *pallias* and a low shaded area with seats. There is a 28-metre long bench covered with black marble next to the high canopy.

◀ (ix) Plaja Pairos: Estacion de Sants (design: Albert Viaplana, Helle Pinori and Ehric Miralles) Pergola (a) night-time; (b) day-time

(a)

(b)

(a)

▲ (x) Jardins de la Villa Cecilia (design: Jose Antonio Martinez Lapena and Elias Torres)
(a) view along path

Jardines de Villa Cecilia, Barcelona

Jose Antonio Martinez Lapena, Elias Torres: Architects

This public park, sponsored by the Urban Projects Service of Barcelona, was completed in 1985. It covers land that formed part of the gardens of Quinta Amelia before the opening of the Santa Amelia road, and it adjoins the gardens of the Villa Cecilia which are now public. The plan reflects the intense speculation about the use of geometry in the open space of the city that was a preoccupation of students in the Barcelona School of Architecture during the 1970s, a factor which tends to override the more functional requirements. The garden is conceived as a series of enjoyable spaces emphasized by different geometric elements. The design of the entrance gates has also been varied to provide interest and orientation. The paving generally is red gravel, different levels being connected by ramps. Planting includes similar species to the adjoining garden, including palm trees, pines, cypresses, lime trees and banana plants. Shrubs enclose and divide different areas, some of which are planted with vegetables.

The Santa Amelia road is screened by a new wall with a door in the centre leading to a metal roof garden of naturalistic design with gigantic leaves of *Gingko biloba* (Maidenhair tree), overlooking the water channel with a sculpture of Ophelia by Francisco Lopez Hernandez.

(b) detail of gates

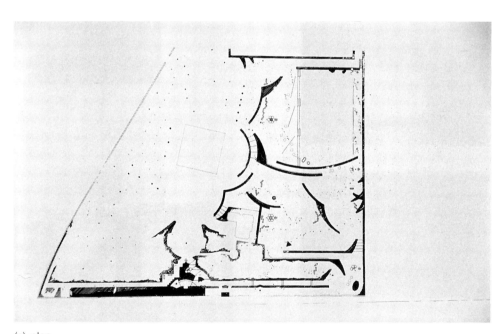

(c) plan

◀ (xi) Jardins de la Unitat (design:
Jordi Farrando). (a) Plan; (b)
general view; (c) detail

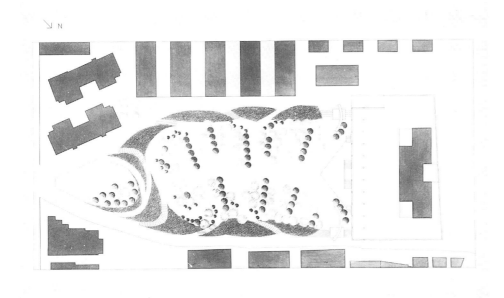

(a)

(b)

(c)

3.8 Neighbourhood park, Merl, Luxembourg

Design: J. and L. Weier de Haas

This is a small recreational park adjoining a school and sports area near to the centre of town. The pool is supplied by the water of a stream, and it is sited in an area which was formerly subject to springtime flooding. There are many different facilities for local residents.

▲ (ii) Winding stream

Figure 3.8 Merl neighbourhood park

▼ (i) View from above

3.9 Urban square, UBS Administration Building, Zurich, Switzerland 1986

Heiner Rodel (landscape architect) in collaboration with
Stephanie Knoblich (landscape architect) and Sergio
Notari (designer)

The new UBS Bank Administration Building is in the commercial and industrial area of Zurich. Together with an adjoining building it forms an irregular forecourt facing a busy street on the north-west side. The design brief was to create an attractive open space focused on the building, combined with a recreation area for the employees. This has been achieved by creating an urban square based upon a grid of lines radiating from the axis of the entrance to the street, which has been turned into an avenue with trees. The square rises up on three levels, devoted to three themes: water, plants and stone, which have been used to make both active and passive spaces.

The stone includes pale grey granite for the steps and framing elements, with quartzite slabs and porphyritic granite setts. Plants include *Robinia pseudacacia* 'Umbraculifera', a variety of shrubs, water plants and areas of grass lawn. Water mirrors the entrance to the building, then flows in channels across the square to two low basins, where the 'Time-Machine' is installed. This has been designed by the artist Ivan Pestalozzi to establish a link between architecture and open space. It is an open steelwork structure 12 m high, from which coloured polyester balls are dropped, one every hour, into a basin – a whimsical expression of the passage of time.

Figure 3.9 Urban square

◄ (i) Entrance

99

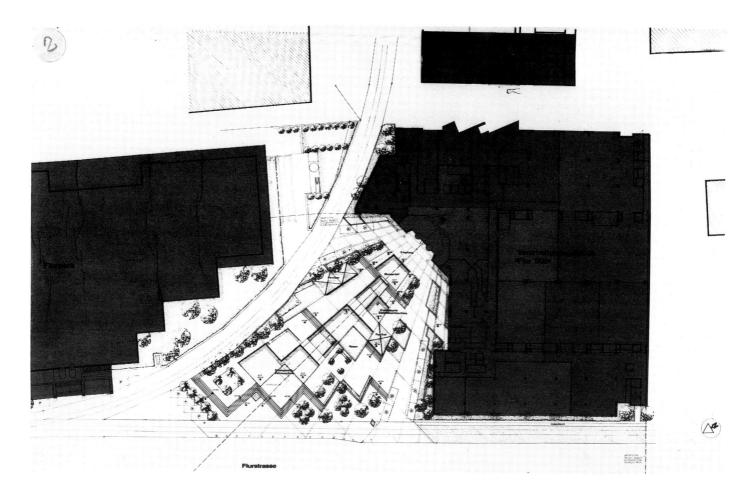

▲ (ii) Plan

◄ (iii) View from above

3.10 Municipal square, Limburg, Maastricht, The Netherlands

Wil Snelder Eys

The main public entrance of the municipal offices in Maastricht, the provincial centre of the province of Limburg, focuses on the square (65 m by 50 m) which is flanked by the two wings of the building. The design for the square follows the 5.4 m grid of the building, but combines it with a new diagonal grid, producing triangles which are either paved or covered with a parterre of clipped box (*Buxus* spp.) and gravel. Although it is principally a traffic-free area, allowance has been made for occasional traffic and fire access to the main entrance to the building and service access to the rear.

Figure 3.10 Maastricht municipal square

◀ (i) Plan

◀ (ii) Fountain with Povinciehuis behind

▼ (iii) General view of square

3.11 Broadgate, London, UK 1986

Arup Associates

The development is a major new financial centre in London extending between Liverpool Street Station and Finsbury Avenue (including a total built area of 150 000 m²) based on a master plan by Arup Associates. The first building comprises offices of eight storeys, with the upper two set back to reduce the scale, permit planting on the balcony roofs, and allow more light into the enclosed square. This is a generally passive space, occasionally used for exhibitions, and lunch-time concerts for office workers. It is paved at its lowest level with open-jointed grey granite setts, surrounded at its upper level by steps and paving in red granite, the material which has also been used for the seats and the fountain. The black façade of the building provides an effective contrast to the plane trees and balcony plants.

The square opens into a second 'active' square which forms the main focus of the development, determined by the movement pattern of pedestrians entering the site from Liverpool Street Station. This is surrounded by shops and restaurants at the lower level and offices at the upper level. These look out over a series of circular planted pergolas on to a circular central space which is used for exhibitions, concerts, and ice-skating in winter. It is faced with travertine in contrast to the pink granite of the surrounding square.

The great success of the scheme is undoubtedly due to the careful planning, segregation of traffic and services underground, the consistently high quality of design and detailing both in the buildings and open spaces, and in the aftercare.

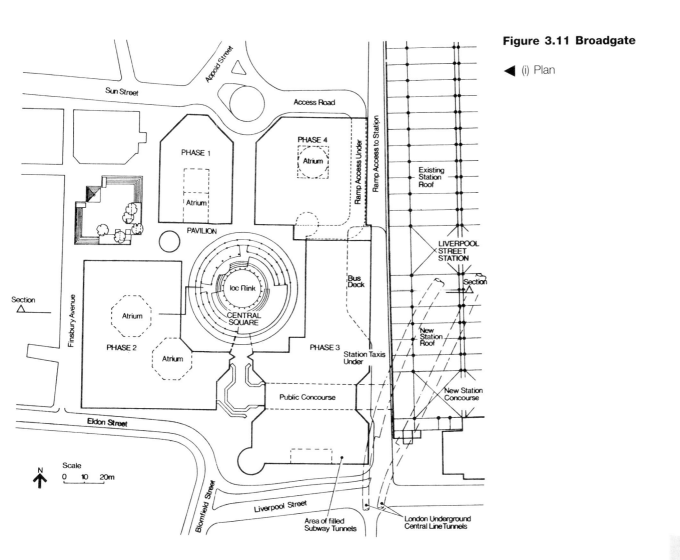

Figure 3.11 Broadgate

◀ (i) Plan

◀ (ii) 'Active' space with circular central area

◀ (iii) 'Passive' square adjoining Finsbury Avenue, with plane trees highlighted against the dark façades of the office buildings

3.12 Grand National Assembly Park and Gardens, Ankara, Turkey

Yüksel Öztan

The design was the subject of a competition held in 1965, for a park and gardens covering an area of 350 000 m² in a residential quarter of Ankara, as designated in the master plan by H. Jansen (1928). The prevailing conditions of the steppe climate, the character of the building complex, the uses of the park and its relationship with the city, were important design considerations determining the division of the site. This includes a garden setting for the approach to the building with public gardens running along the length of the Ataturk Bulvari, and a further garden built on a hill for viewing the city. More than 200 species of trees and shrubs have been planted.

Figure 3.12 Grand National Assembly park and gardens

◀ (i) Public promenade

◀ (ii) Fountain

APPLIED COLOUR

The earliest adaptations of colour by human beings were almost certainly in the adornment of the body: by painting, tattooing, and dressing with feathers, jewellery and clothing. From this it was but a short step to the symbolism and sympathetic magic that we call *art*. The extraordinary groups of animals depicted in the caves at Lascaux and Altamira (*c.* 30 000–10 000 BC) have been described as 'the first landscapes' (Jellicoe and Jellicoe, 1975). Adaptation has continued functionally in ceremonial adornment, badges, signs and traffic lights; also more indiscriminately in advertising and decoration of all kinds.

Traditional uses of colour on buildings are many and varied, particularly in places where colour has been used for other purposes, such as painting boats. The choice of colours was, on the whole, determined by precedent and conditioned by availability and cost, rather than individual expression. The strongest influences until the nineteenth century, were those of the court and the aristocracy. In the nineteenth century the uses of colour were greatly extended in all fields: scientific, industrial, architectural and artistic. The work begun by Chevreul in the 1830s was complemented by the synthesization of colours in the 1860s, and both exerted a significant influence on Impressionist painting. From the few hundred colours that had been generally available, the number that could be manufactured from petroleum products had increased, by 1980, to approximately three million, of which nine thousand were actually in production. Although the effect upon the clothing and textile industries has been dramatic, it has been relatively slow in terms of the environment, until recently. One reason in Britain was Ruskin's stricture concerning the honesty of self-coloured materials, which has survived to the present. Very large buildings were regarded as monuments, even if they were power stations, such as those at Battersea and Bankside in London. But their intrusion into the countryside in the post-war years has generated much opposition, which has given rise to various strategies for disguise and concealment, including the use of colour.

Camouflage in nature depends upon both pattern and colour. The function of the pattern is to break the outlines of the body at rest in the background. Where the background is simple – for example in land seen from above – simple landscape colours can make the object or building invisible. But this is rarely appropriate for buildings seen from the ground. For these, the combinations of land camouflage and sea camouflage techniques are more appropriate. The latter include 'dazzle painting', a development of Vorticism, applied by a group of artists to battleships during the First World War. The forms of the battleships were broken up with patterns of colours relating to the sea and sky, to give the illusion that they were steaming in different directions. Applications to buildings range from the simple use of colours selected for their landscape affinity to the *distractive* breaking up of large surfaces by means of variably 'advancing' and 'retreating' colours. The first has been used to great effect at Winfrith in Dorset, where the effects of the colours have been carefully gauged to suit the distance from which they are seen; the second at Fawley in Hampshire.

The colours used in both cases are local: those of Fawley – including the orange accent colours of the doors – are derived from the local shingle, and those of Winfrith from the surrounding heathland vegetation. The distractive method has also been used for the aircraft hanger at Stansted, but in this case the achromatic colours have been selected primarily to 'work' with the sky. At Partington, both techniques have been employed: the graduated bands of red and purple adding decorative interest as well as relating to the adjoining urban landscape colours. The use of colour in urban areas is rarely simple; they are often dominated by commercial considerations. The yellow Renault house colour which Norman Foster chose for the depot at Swindon was perfectly related to the landscape (see Lancaster, 1984), but not at all to the coloured buildings that have since surrounded it. In the case of the industrial depot at Granite Wharf, the yellow house colour of Wimpey Hobbs has been chosen for the signs and the 'working parts' – cranes and conveyors – which has made them appropriately conspicuous landmarks on the Greenwich riverside, in contrast to the modified blue of the buildings which merges easily into the background.

Aircraft hangar, Stansted Airport, UK (design: Faulks, Perry, Culley and Rech).

Although the upper half of this lozenge-shaped building is always seen against the skyline, attempts to imitate 'sky blue' were regarded as pointless. Instead the achromatic silver and white were chosen as 'colours' that would blend with the whitish sky that is common in Britain for much of the year. These have been applied – together with slate grey at the lower levels – in blocks to break up the visual effect of mass and to emphasize the horizontality. Narrow bands of dark blue have been used as accent colour

▲ (i) Distant view

▼ (ii) View towards entrance showing the different effects of sunlight and shadow on the coloured panels

▲ (i) Middle distance view of Zebra building showing how the reds merge into the heath landscape

▲ (ii) In the near view the reds appear in strong contrast to the bright green of the mown grass

▲ (iii) The close-up reveals how brilliant edge colours have been used to sharpen the image of the building

Winfrith Technology Centre, UK (colour design: Nicholas Pearson Associates)

Winfrith Technology Centre is owned by AEA (Atomic Energy Association) Technology. It was one of the first sites developed in the mid 1950s to carry out research into experimental nuclear reactors, located in a large area of Dorset heathland. The proposed rehabilitation of the buildings was approved by the planning authority subject to the submission of a code of practice for future development and approval of a detailed scheme for their integration with the site. This was undertaken by Nicholas Pearson Associates.

Two aims were identified: to integrate the buildings with the site when seen from a distance, and to improve their visual image at close quarters. A series of colour studies were made from different positions in the surrounding landscape, which included mixed farmland, broadleaf woodland, coniferous woodland, heathland and parkland. Colour boards were made and tested on site, allowing for seasonal changes. These provided the basis for a palette, from which a colour strategy was prepared, aimed specifically at reducing the effect of 'clutter' in the middle areas, and emphasizing some of the smaller elements. Strong colours were suggested by the heath landscape, including the pinks and purples of heather, vivid yellow of gorse, and bracken changing from bright green to flame red – all seen against the duller browns and greens of the distant landscape. Applied to the Zebra building, the selected colours of dark red, orange-yellow and dark brown, highlighted with bright pink, appear fresh and lively in the near view; but in the middle and far distance, they blend very effectively with the landscape

▲ (i) Close-up view

▲ (ii) View from middle distance across water

Fawley Power Station, UK (design: Farmer and Dark).

Applications of colour derived from 'dazzle painting' or camouflage techniques can be very effective in reducing the effect of bulk. In this example the almost achromatic greys, white and black, including the orange accent of colour of the doors, were suggested by the colours of the shingle. It is interesting in itself, it distracts from the 'clutter' of the surroundings, and the colours relate well to the changing colours of sea and sky

Tanks at Partington, UK (design: Faulks, Perry, Culley and Rech (formerly Architects Design Group)).

The designers have added an expressive dimension to their use of colour to reduce the effect of bulking. The tanks have been painted with graded vertical banding in red, purple, white and silver, relating differently to the three types of associated landscape; rural, industrial and residential

▲ (i) View of newly coloured buildings and plant

Greenwich riverside, Granite Wharf, UK (colour design: Michael Lancaster).

The aerial view looking towards the north from the area of Greenwich Palace and Power Station reveals both the importance of colour and the need for a co-ordinated colour policy for the Thames riverside. The newly completed colour scheme for the Wimpey Hobbs plant at Granite Wharf, approved by the London borough of Greenwich, can be seen in the middle of the picture.

The clients were offered a range of 17 main colours and 10 accent colours for the cladding of their plant. After consideration, these were reduced to four pairs of combinations that would 'work' with the yellow house colour of the company. From these, the modified blue was accepted as being the most appropriate for the 'static' buildings to relate to the river and the site, with bright yellow for the 'working parts'. These will provide a strong focal point contrasted with the blue which will recede into the background (unlike the greenish-blue which has been used further downstream)

▲ (ii) Aerial view showing Granite Wharf in the riverside context

CHAPTER 4

Landscapes of memory

Time present and time past/ Are both perhaps present in time future/
And time future contained in time past/ If all time is eternally present/
All time is unredeemable.
Footfalls echo in the memory/ Down the passage we did not take/
Towards the door we never opened/ Into the rose garden.
(T.S. Eliot, *Burnt Norton*)

All landscapes are, in a sense, landscapes of memory. Our first discoveries of nature and our surroundings become imprinted on our memories. Memory also becomes sanctified by society in a number of different ways. The most obvious of these is in the religious ceremonies and institutions associated with birth, puberty, marriage and death, all aspects of personal and family history, the last of which is recorded in monuments. Typically, these 'rites of passage' are symbolized by gateways – layers of access in the form of rooms or enclosures – through which it is necessary for the initiates to pass. The traditional English church has a sequence beginning at the lynchgate, passing through the graveyard, into the porch; from the porch it extends along the aisle to the chancel, and finally to the sanctuary. Whether or not the religious feelings are still strong, it is these sacred places – churches, chapels, synagogues, mosques – which give focus to a community. In them, the history of places is written; and they themselves are evidence of much longer spans of history which lead us back into the remote past.

Burial sites were among the first gathering places in which settlements grew and there are many cases in which continuity is expressed in layers of prehistory and history overlaid – where Christian communities sought either to engage or suppress those of pre-Christian religion. This occurs at Old Sarum near Salisbury where a church was built inside an Iron Age fort; at Avebury in Wiltshire where the whole village straddles the Bronze Age Stone circle; at Carnac in Brittany where crosses have been inscribed on standing

stones, and in Portugal where dolmens were converted into chapels in the seventeenth century.

The continuity of history is not always so neatly expressed, nor are the monuments treated so reverently. The Roman temple which stands at the centre of Evora in Portugal was used as a slaughter-house until the nineteenth century, and the Parthenon was an explosives store under Turkish rule – perhaps not an entirely unsuitable use for a temple dedicated to a Goddess of War.

The expression of continuity becomes more challenging when the succeeding buildings are of different periods, or new – as in Nîmes where the Carrée d'Art is sited alongside the Maison Carrée. The choice of materials, paving and street furniture has to work for both. In the case of the Acropolis area in Athens, the range of considerations is expanded beyond that of buildings and street furniture to include natural topography and the fickle medium of plants.

Large rural sites present particular problems arising from a conflict between land-use and public access, especially where the site is unmanned. In the case of White Horse Hill this involved many years of landscape and agricultural planning with only a minimum of design intervention in the siting of the car park below the line of the hill-slope. The formerly isolated stone circle of Stonehenge has had to be rescued from an earlier crude 'interpretative' development with underground buildings and exposed car park, by a new design competition, currently under consideration. The increasing demand for public access has to be balanced against the vulnerability of any site. Even signs are likely to be detrimental in certain cases.

Historical buildings present opportunities both for enhancement and for the negation of their historical value. A simple approach has been adopted in Volterra, by providing a park to emphasize the relationship between the castle and the town. For the Villa Pucci, the continuous angled steps provide a link with the present and its Renaissance origins. In the case of the Villa Roseto, the latter effect has been achieved by the creation of a new garden by Pietro Porcinai, which echoes the qualities of the surrounding landscape. Attempts at reproduction, even if they are practicable, must be seen as inferior to such creative approaches.

The historical significance of places impinges subtly on our senses. Kevin Lynch asks: 'What time is this place?', referring not merely to the embodiment of history, but also to the expression of time in materials and movement patterns (Lynch 1972). Patterns and alignments can determine whether paths are fast or slow, and materials can express time in a variety of ways: the material itself, its durability and the way it is used, are all significant. The boulders used in Mariebjerg Cemetery and the carved stones in Novo Žale are important expressions of geological time, just as trees and plants are living expressions of time passing.

Figure 4.1 White Horse Hill

(i) One of the earliest landscapes, an aerial view of the white horse cut in the chalk, the Iron Age hill fort, Uffington Castle, and the patterns of strip lynchetts revealed by the low sun. The new car park is off the picture to the right

4.1 White Horse Hill, Oxfordshire, UK

Colvin and Moggridge (for the Compton Beauchamp Estates)

Uffington Castle and White Horse Hill form the highest point on the Berkshire Downs and a prominent landmark in the Upper Thames Valley. They lie within the 6000 acre Compton Beauchamp Estate, in Oxfordshire.

By the early 1960s managers of the Estate realized that the area around the Horse and Castle was becoming over used: the monuments were being damaged, the car park was obtrusive and inadequate, and congestion on access roads conflicted with agriculture, especially during harvest. Earlier management agreements between the landowner and the old Ministry of Public Buildings and Works had become inadequate as more open grass downland was ploughed and increasing car ownership brought more visitors.

▲ (ii) Long section showing the relationship between the white horse and the new car park

▼ (iii) Plan

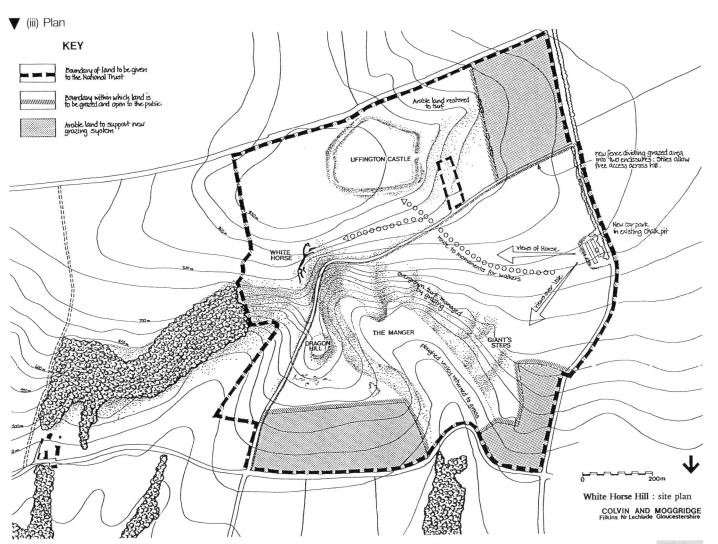

KEY

- Boundary of land to be given to the National Trust
- Boundary within which land is to be grazed and open to the public
- Arable land to support new grazing system

White Horse Hill : site plan
COLVIN AND MOGGRIDGE
Filkins Nr Lechlade Gloucestershire

In order to integrate agriculture and recreation it was necessary to increase the area open to the public (from 35 to 230 acres) by recreating downland grass grazed by sheep. This principle was identified early in the project, in agreement with the Estate's managing agents, and a layout was agreed. In this way pressure on the monuments was reduced, and their setting was improved by siting a new car park in an old chalk pit away from the Castle. Former arable land was taken in hand and regrassed with a seed mix designed to match the colour of the old turf. Advice from the Nature Consevancy Council was sought to achieve an open swrd for gradual recolonization by herb species from the adjoining old chalk turf, while at the same time providing sufficient keep for the sheep. Derelict grassland was reclaimed for grazing on the Giants' Steps and Dragon Hill.

The costs of re-fencing and the car park were grant-aided by the Countryside Commission. Following the reorganization, the site was handed to the National Trust, who have continued the reinstatement of eroded grassland. The project received an Europa Nostra Award in 1979 and was a BBC Design Award finalist in 1987.

4.2 Volterra Park, Pisa, Italy

Marco Pozzoli: Landscape Architect

The project to provide an appropriate parkland setting for the Medici Fort and the archaeological excavations of the Roman baths in Pisa was supported by a local bank. In respect of the objective the designer has opted for minimal intervention. This included the creation of a large informal amphitheatre with a small road curving along the edge, and indigenous planting comprising Holm oak, laurel and cypress.

Figure 4.2 Volterra Park
View towards the Medici Fort and part of the old town across the new park with the path running up the side

4.3 Villa Pucci, Florence, Italy

Design: Gae Auli Aulenti: Architect

The addition of continuous angled steps in concrete and grass helps to 'fix' the Florentine villa on the site and at the same time provides a link with the swimming pool among the trees at the bottom.

Figure 4.3 Villa Pucci

▼ (i),

▼ (ii) The relationship between the villa and the landscape is redefined by the angled concrete steps which lead the eye down to the swimming pool among the trees at the bottom of the garden

(iii) Plan ▶

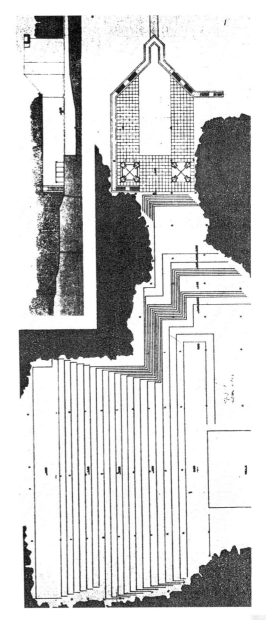

4.4 Villa Roseto, Florence, Italy 1962

Pietro Porcinai: Landscape Architect

In this private Florentine garden Porcinai demonstrates his profound attachment to the classical Renaissance garden tradition as well as a sensitivity to the qualities of the hilly landscape. The broad clipped hedge acts both as an effective boundary and an indicator of the slope of the hill.

◀ Figure 4.4 Villa Roseto
Two views of Pietro Porecinai's design for the garden of the Villa Roseto. The hedge emphasizes the slope of the hill and the serpentine path introduces new perspectives

4.5 Piazza San Giulio, Varese, Italy 1986

Gilberto Oneto

The design brief was to provide a focus for the church and a centre (*parvis*) for religious processions, public ceremonies and social meetings in this small village of Varese in the densely populated area to the north of Milan. The small square (3000 square m) had formerly been used for car parking. There were no buildings of outstanding architectural quality apart from the church. The importance of the church has been emphasized by a short flight of steps and the paving pattern, which forms an extension to the access road. The axis thus created divides the square into two areas: a raised meeting space furnished with an old monument and a small parking area, both defined by planting. The walls and seats are built of reinforced concrete; kerbs, steps and the grid pattern of the square are of granite; and the infill paving of porphyry setts. The trees are *Celtis australis* and shrubs include: *Rhodedendron spp.*, Azalea japonica, and *Cotoneaster salicifolia.*

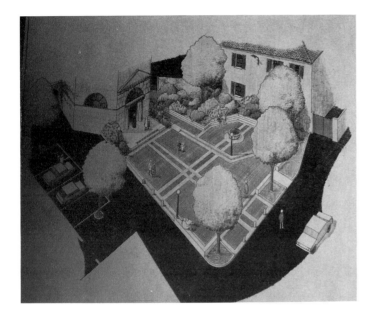

Figure 4.5 Piazza San Giulio

◀ (i) Aerial perspective showing the piazza as proposed ten years after completion

▼ (ii) View over the lower part of the square to the church with the fields beyond

4.6 Eyüp Mosque, Istanbul, Turkey

G. Akdoğan

Until the middle of the eighteenth century the Golden Horn and the district of Eyüp were famous for their summer houses with garden pavilions. Neglect and the growth of industries were responsible for a long period of decline. In 1985 a project was launched to restore the Golden Horn to its former beauty. This involved clearing the industries from the shores, establishing green open spaces for the city dwellers, and restoring historic religious centres, such as the Eyüp Mosque.

The site is named after the Muslim saint Eyüp, who was a symbol of patience and tolerance, and a close friend of the prophet Mohammed. Obeying a command from the Koran, he came to Istanbul with an army of thousands and after fighting a battle outside the city walls, died in AD 672. In AD 1422 Sultan Mehmet II built a religious complex – including a mosque, tombs, a refectory and a school – on the presumed site of his grave. It became customary for Ottoman Sultans to pay a visit on accession to the throne, and it has become one of the most frequently visited sites for receiving blessings, fulfilling vows and making wishes.

The main objectives of the project, which was carried out in three stages, were: to accommodate religious ceremonies, visitors from the country and from overseas; to provide for tourists and for the local population. This involved the diversion of traffic, the demolition and clearance of irrelevant buildings, and changes of use to buildings of historical significance. It included the provision of a central square linked by steps and ramps to a series of smaller squares and spaces for a range of activities from reading, playing chess, listening to religious music and contemplation, to children's play and the buying of local handicrafts. The design aims were to provide contemporary solutions to problems while reflecting Turkish – Islamic traditions. This has been achieved by the use of fountains and pools of marble and granite, with benches covered in white mosaic, specially designed lamps, and waste receptacles. Trees such as plane, ash, lime, oak and cypress – all favoured by the Ottoman Emperors – have been planted; with a concession to more recent tastes for colour in flower beds surrounded by box hedges.

Figure 4.6 Eyup Mosque
▼ (i) Plan

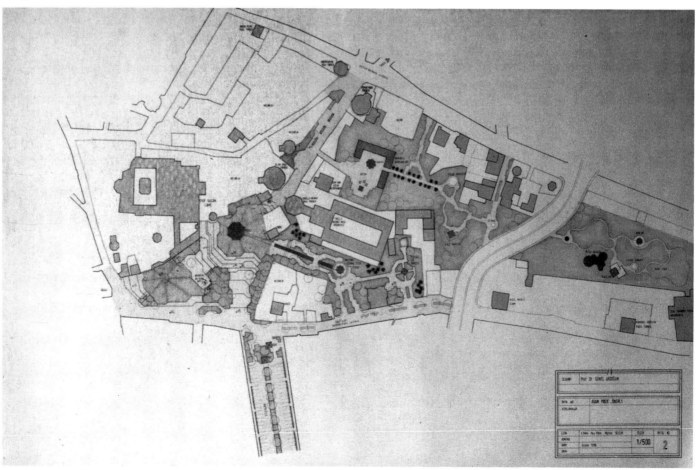

◀ (ii) Mosque with new courtyard

◀ (iii) Mosque and graveyard with new fountain in foreground

4.7 La Place du Carrée, Nîmes, France 1991–2

Sir Norman Foster and Partners/Ville de Nîmes

The design commission for the Carrée d'Art in Nîmes won in an international design competition, provided the opportunity for the development, initially, of the Place relating the new building to the Maison Carrée, built by the Roman architect Crispius Reberrus in AD 27; subsequently, of the streets connecting it to the other monuments of the old city. A new forum has been created around the temple, with steps descending from

Figure 4.7 La Place du Carrée

◀ (i) View of the Carrée d'Art with the Maison Carrée in the foreground

◀ (ii) View of completed square and Maison Carrée from the Carrée d'Art

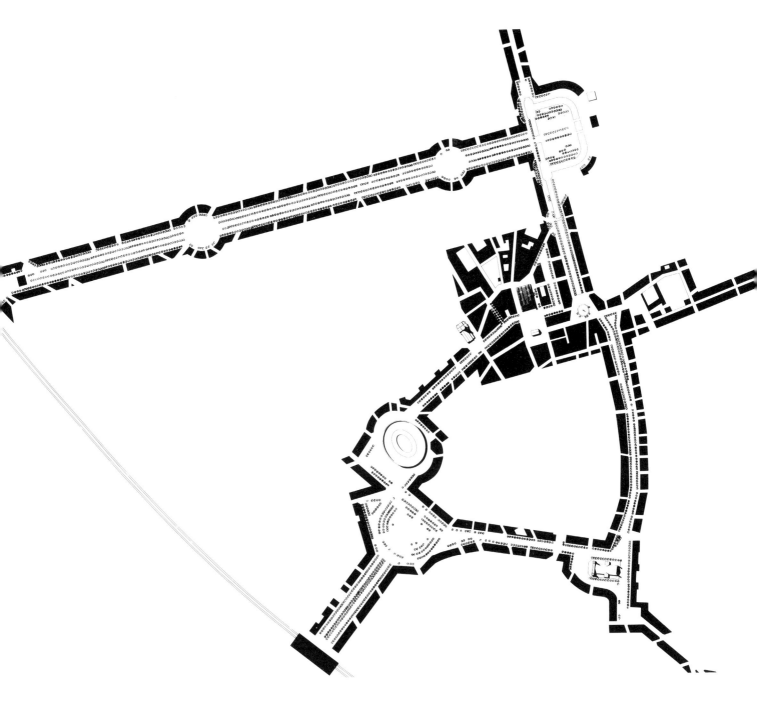

▲ (iii) Master plan showing the relationship of the Place du Carrée with the other monuments in the old city

the present to the Roman level, following the line of the original peristyle demolished in the nineteenth century. By contrast, the Carrée d'Art sits on a 1.8 m high podium – highly articulated with steps and ramps for disabled – to protect the building from the threat of flooding.

After extensive research into stonework, both in terms of material and labour, it was decided to adopt two methods. The thick grey granite blocks of the roads is the work of stone-masons and paviors; for the fine, delicately-shaped beige limestone of the pedestrian areas associated with the buildings, monumental masons were employed. The enormous difficulty of combining new with old, which is so often defeated by public opinion as well as technical incompetence, has been achieved with great elegance.

4.8 The Acropolis Archaeological Area, Athens, Greece

Dimitri Pikionis

Figure 4.8 The Acropolis Archaeological Area

▼ (i) Road and footpath study for the landscape design of the area immediately below the Acropolis

▲ (ii) paved area with the Acropolis in the background

Dimitri Pikionis, Professor of Architecture at the Athens Polytechic, was commissioned in 1951 to undertake a general improvement for the principal archaeological sites, in cooperation with the Greek National Tourist Organisation. Pikionis had been 'emotionally involved' with the Attic landscape since his schooldays, believing that 'nature was invested with deep metaphysical significance – a religious spirit' which prompted him to fight against any intrusive development which he saw as damaging (Pikionis, 1935).

The project included analytical studies and replanning of the following areas: the Acropolis, the Hills of the Muses (Philopappou Hill), the Hill of the Nymphs (Observatory Hill), and the design of a pavilion adjoining the small church of St Dimitri Loumbardiaris, and improvements to the church itself and the priests' house. The working brief is described by Pikionis:

The architect will have to devise new methods of dealing with every aspect of the work down to the last detail; he will have to revise all building methods currently in use and invest them with the validity of practices inspired by ancient art ../ . the construction of way-stations, pavilions etc., will require stones of a special texture, shape and colour, as well as large loose boulders and marble lintels from ancient or neo-classical buildings. Reliefs and capitals will be ensconced in the walls. The alleyways and pathways will be ornamented with antique fragments, such as stone benches and cylindrical shapes belonging to tombs from the period of Dimitri Poliorcetes, which can be found in abundance in the courtyard of the National Archaeological Museum. Several other antique fragments discovered 'insitu' will also be used for this purpose.

Pikionis goes on to specify the types of materials, including wood for new timber structures, which should either be in its natural state, or processed in such a way as to be in keeping with the spirit of the project. With regard to vegetation, he stipulated a special study of the 'visual, chromatic, formal and symbolic aspects of trees and shrubs on the site, as well as the overall landscape composition, and new planting near to the ancient monuments should be of indigenous species such as laurels, myrtles and pomegranates, like those which originally adorned the sanctuaries.' He recommended the removal of non-indigenous trees altogether, and others, such as cypresses, should be limited because their columnar forms tend to reduce the visual impact of columns.

In no sense is this historical reproduction: it is an essay in careful adaptation to the old and integration of the new. The immense care and attention to detail, exercised by Pikionis and his team, have resulted in one of the most perfect man-made landscapes of the period.

 (iii) paving, steps and planting

◄ (iv) Detail of stonework

(v) The old and the new; view through the pavilion of St Dimitri Loumbardiaris towards the Acropolis

(vi) sketch by architect

4.9 Odeion of Herodius Atticus, Athens, Greece 1960–61

Alexander Papageorgiou-Venetas: Architect and Planning Consultant

Spyro Lembessis: Landscape Architect

Figure 4.9 Odeion of Herodius Atticus

◀ (i) Aerial view of the Roman theatre and the Eumenis stoa on the south side of the Acropolis

▼ (ii) Plan showing the steps leading to the Roman theatre

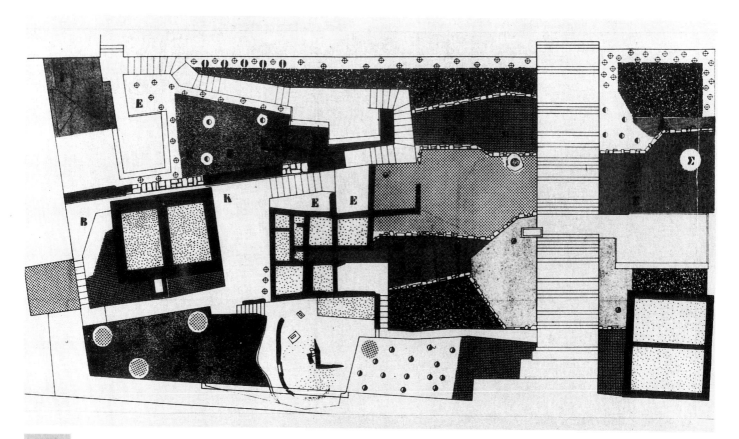

At the conclusion of work to the Acropolis Archaeological Area in Athens by Dimitri Pikionis, the Curator Ioannis Miliadis commissioned the redesign of the excavation area in front of the Odeion (Roman theatre) on the slope of the Acropolis rock. The aim was to provide public access for the first time to three important sites of antiquities: the water cisterns of the Roman theatre, the archaic temple of the Nymphs, and the ruins of newly discovered Hellenistic houses. These were carefully integrated into the new design.

(iii) Detail of the steps leading to the excavation area ▶

4.10 Park in Kefalari-Kifissia, Athens, Greece 1958

Alexander Papageorgiou-Venetos: Architect and Planning Consultant

Spyro Tsaoussis: Landscape Architect

P. Vassiliadis: Architect and City Planner (Ministry of Housing, Athens)

Generations of Athenians have walked and played around the 'water' of Kefallari, one of the finest northern suburbs of the capital. The water comes from a well 30–50 m deep, which supplies the famous cistern and the gardens of Kifissia, situated near to the two churches, the Church of the Metamorphosis (Transfiguration) and the Church of St Sotiris. Together they occupy a space of about 150 by 95 m, shaded with pine trees.

In 1958 the Greek Tourist Organization promoted the redesign of the area to include a new water reservoir in the form of a small lake controlled by three pumps (two old ones and a new one underground), a coffee shop, and a pavilion containing a cigarette kiosk, two telephone booths and a flower shop.

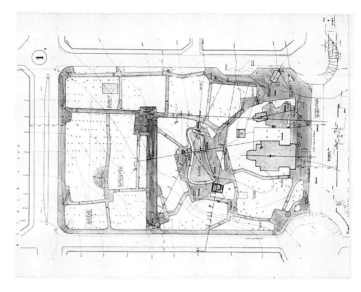

Figure 4.10 Park in Kefalari-Kifissia

▲ (i) Plan

▲ (ii) General view

(iii) Detail of paving and fountain adjoining the old church ▶

4.11 Central Athens pedestrian system, Greece

Anastasia Remundu-Triantafyllis: Architect and City Planner (Ministry of Environment and Regional Planning)

Marina Chaidopoulou-Adams: Landscape Architect – Consultant

In 1978 a detailed study was undertaken for the pedestrianization of central Athens. The aim was to segregate vehicle and pedestrian circulation and to link the latter to the green spaces associated with the Acropolis, Lycabettus Hill and other archaeological sites. Initially restricted to the area of Plaka old town, the project was later extended to the commercial centre of Athens, and it included areas that had been upgraded by teams of architects and planners in the 'Special Services' department of the Ministry of Regional Planning and Environment. (Planning and construction was taken over by the Department of The Reorganisation of Free Public Open Spaces, under the Direction of K. Pavlopoulos, 1978–82, and continued from 1983–90 by the Ministry of Planning and Environment under Director F. Karassavidou.) Some schemes were awarded to private practices (as in the case of Metropolis Square by A. Tombazis Associates) and some were the subject of competitions.

Figure 4.11 Central Athens pedestrian system

▼ (i) General plan

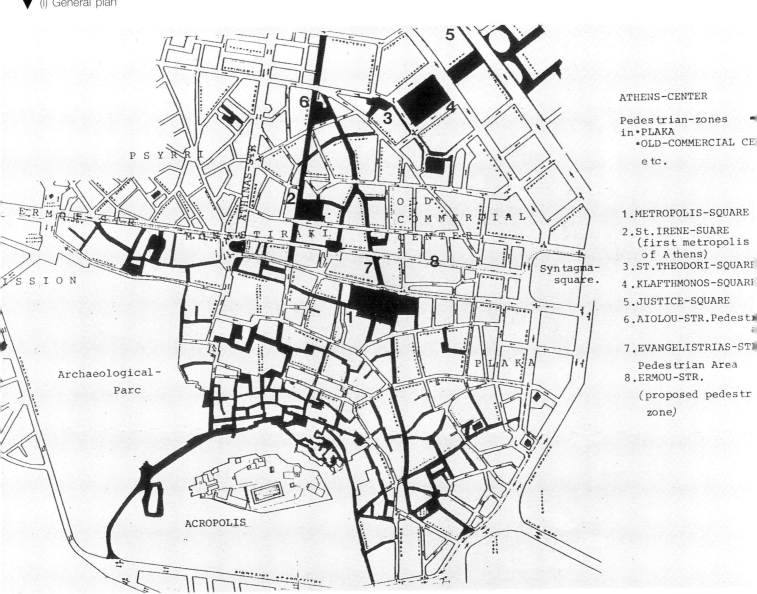

ATHENS-CENTER

Pedestrian-zones
in •PLAKA
   •OLD-COMMERCIAL CE

etc.

1. METROPOLIS-SQUARE
2. St.IRENE-SUARE
   (first metropolis
   of Athens)
3. ST.THEODORI-SQUARE
4. KLAFTHMONOS-SQUARE
5. JUSTICE-SQUARE
6. AIOLOU-STR.Pedestr
7. EVANGELISTRIAS-STR
   Pedestrian Area
8. ERMOU-STR.
   (proposed pedestr
   zone)

Materials were chosen for their affinity to the Attic environment. These included marble paving of different sizes, colours and textures, brick paviors and concrete setts (which relate well in colour generally). Similarly, indigenous planting was favoured, including: cypress, olive, lemon, plane and *Citrus aurantium*. But other,

ornamental, species such as *Brachychiton acerifolium*, *Cercis siliquastrum*, *Jacaranda mimosifolia* and *Populus alba*, as well as various deciduous shrubs have been used to enrich existing public spaces. These have become popular meeting-places and islands of seclusion in a city that suffers seriously from pollution.

▼ (ii) Metropolis Square (a) view from above showing paving

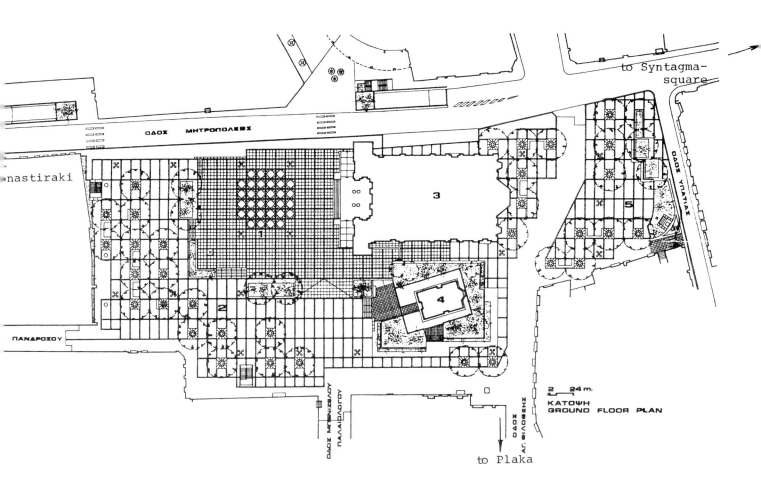

ΟΔΟΣ ΜΗΤΡΟΠΟΛΕΩΣ

nastiraki

ΠΑΝΔΡΟΣΟΥ

1

2

3

4

5

to Syntagma-square

ΟΔΟΣ ΥΠΑΤΙΑΣ

2   24 m.

ΚΑΤΟΨΗ
GROUND FLOOR PLAN

to Plaka

▲ (b) plan

▶ (c) Detail of paving in the square

▼ (d) St Eleftherius Church adjoining the Metropolis cathedral
after completion of work

127

▲ (iii) St Theodori Square (design: I. Danou, G. Kandiloros, E. Pyrgiotis and A. Remundu; consultant: Marina Adams) Church surrounded by commercial centre

▼ (iv) Klafthmonos Square (design: Seva Karakosta; construction: Ministry of Regional Planning). Integration of the ancient wall into the landscape

▲ (v) Justice Square (design: Ministry of Regional Planning and Athens Polytechnic School)

▼ (vi) Evangelistrias Street (design: A. Remundu-Triantafyllis and E. Pyrgiotis, Urban Design Directorate, Ministry of Regional Planning). Detail of new landscape looking towards Metropolis Square

CEMETERIES

The modern cemetery began to develop as a response to the overcrowding in cities at the beginning of the nineteenth century. There were pressures of two kinds. Sanitary reformers objected to the increasingly speedy disinterment of bodies to make space for more, and religious minorities campaigned for burial grounds and services that were not limited to members of the established church. Paris set a precedent banning churchyard burial in 1804, and in the same year land was set aside for the cemetery of Père-Lachaise. During the 1820s and 1830s non-denominational cemeteries began to appear in England in three basic styles: landscape, formal and transitional. By the 1840s, simple geometrical layouts were becoming common because of their convenience for setting out graves (Blackett, 1986). In the present century in Britain convenience has become the predominant factor in layouts that appear to be determined more by the needs of the gang-mower than by any aesthetic considerations. But, as Frances Clegg has suggested, the overall design of the cemetery is probably less important for the average mourner than the appearance of the individual grave (Clegg, 1989).

In many cities, cemeteries were provided before public parks, thereby performing dual functions, either in the inner areas or in the suburbs. Lawn cemeteries developed in an unbroken tradition from those advocated by Downing in North America in the 1840s, after J.C. Loudon. The simple device of placing graves and markers flush with the grass permits large areas of virtually uninterrupted grassland, thereby facilitating maintenance. The forest and woodland cemetery has had a more limited application, relying as it does upon relatively mature woodland and low burial densities: a situation prevailing in northern Europe and Scandinavia. Design competitions have produced some outstanding combinations of both types: notably, the forst cemetery at Enskede near Stockholm by Asplund and Lewerentz and the Mariebjerg Cemetery in Copenhagen by G.N. Brandt and his successors. In the first, constructed between 1917 and 1940, on the site of old gravel pits, Christian symbolism plays an important part in the processional Way of the Cross which has been dramatically integrated into the hillside. At Mariebjerg, the gently sloping rectangular site was planted with woodland trees ten years before development, to achieve a semblance of maturity. This cemetery is non-denominational, providing a range of different burial and memorial possibilities, the design and management of which are supervised by the Director who is also a Landscape Architect.

The northern woodland tradition is now gaining popularity even in southern Europe where land is available, on the grounds of cost, social equality, and where appropriate, religion. This has been adopted by Niko Stare as an alternative design to the 'classical formality' of that originally proposed in the small town of Vuzenica near Dravograd, close to the Austrian border of Slovenia. In Holland the cemetery park form has been developed in Almere-Haven (1974), where the high water table and the flat landscape have been overriding factors in the design. The raised leaf-like lobes of this open complex can be adopted for burial as required.

The architectural cemetery – the necropolis or 'City of the Dead' – belongs more to the civic tradition of southern Europe, demanding high densities. Carlo Scarpa has followed the tradition in his private tomb for the Brion family, but has carefully reconsidered the design of every item, from the wall to the tomb, and incorporated a small water garden which is alternatively introverted and reaching out to the 'borrowed landscape' of the village and mountains beyond. A similar approach has been adopted in Marco Music's extension to the cemetery built by Jose Plecnik before the war. In this City of the Dead classicism has been pared down almost to abstraction by the use of Platonic solid forms, enriched by the expressive grain and colour of natural stone. Like that of the Brion Tomb, the detail is rich in symbolism, which is expressed also in related landscape elements such as the soft outlines of the grass mounds.

As most western economies are faced with increasing costs and declining standards of maintenance, at the same time as the populations increase and the demand for dedicated burial space increases, new solutions are necessary. Christopher Alexander suggests fragmentation, or the dedication of small burial grounds which could become the focal points of different ethnic and religious communities, thereby reinforcing their sense of community. (Alexander, 1977). In Britain, drastic measures are needed to reintegrate the large urban cemeteries that are rapidly falling into dereliction, into effectively co-ordinated systems of urban open space.

4.12 Mariebjerg Park Cemetery, Gentofte, Copenhagen, Denmark

Design: G.N. Brandt: Landscape Architect (for original cemetery)

Morton Falmer-Nielsen: Landscape Architect and Director

Figure 4.12 Mariebjerg Park Cemetery

▼ (i) Revised plan

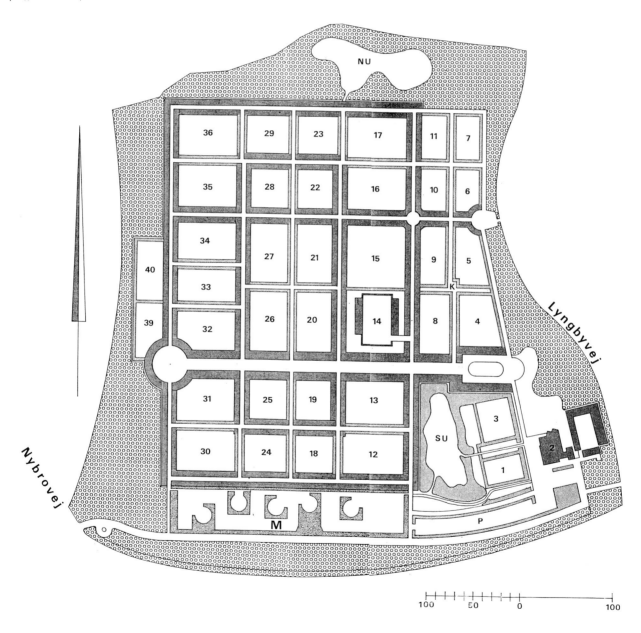

▲ (ii) View from entrance area showing how ground sculpture
has been used to catch the light

◄ (iii) Detail of granite sett path leading through the woodland
towards the light

The Copenhagen cemetery park originally designed by
G.N. Brandt was opened in 1936 after an interval of ten
years to allow the trees to attain a measure of maturity.
These are arranged in avenues of different species to
give identity to the different areas of the grid plan. The
site provides for burial, cremation and for urn burial in
alternative locations – in a woodland dell, in areas of
lawn, or in rectangular enclosures with high or low
hedges.

Priorities have changed over the years and there has
been an increased demand for urn burial in the vicin-
ity of the buildings, with the result that the more
distant areas are neglected by the public and liable to
vandalism. The changes have been undertaken with
skill and sensitivity by the Landscape Architect Morton
Falmer-Nielsen, who is also the current director.

(iv) A traditional regional detail has been adapted in the use of granite boulders to support a hedge bank screening the road; the boulders are not only decorative, but they convey a sense of geological time

◄ (v) Grave plots surrounded by clipped hedges of different heights limit the permitted heights and the variety of planting and the ornaments within helping to unify the area

4.13 Cemetery Almere-Haven, The Netherlands

Christian Zalm, Dienst Stedebouw and Volkshuisvesting

Almere-Haven adjoins Almere New Town in the western part of the polder Zuidelijk Flevoland, which was reclaimed from the Ysselmeer in 1968. The Structure Plan (1974) showed a small town with a projected population growth to 20 000 inhabitants over ten years, with amenities to be phased in over the development period. The first cluster of houses was accompanied by the building of a supermarket, a café, a church and the cemetery, all grouped around the centre of the town near the harbour.

The cemetery was established on the sand-layer behind the dyke at the edge of Lake Gooimeer, near to the harbour and the first group of houses, opposite the church. It was conceived as a public park containing secluded areas which can be added to the cemetery when necessary, thus expressing the passage of time and the unity of life and death in a small community. A public cycle path between the town centre and the eastern housing areas, divides the cemetery into two parts, both of which are raised up 2 m to keep them

Figure 4.13 Cemetery Almere-Haven

▼ (i) Aerial view showing the town and harbour

▲ (ii) View of path

above the water-table and to segregate them from the public areas. At present, they are enclosed by hedges of *Acer campestre*, *Ulmus europaeus* and *Tilia tomentosa*, with open entrances. Later, when the areas are used for burials, fences will be provided. These areas are linked by a small road to the meeting hall where mourners take leave of the bodies and ashes of the dead. In the centre there is a small public park with seats, shrubs and flowers. Apart from the grass, the planting generally is all deciduous, comprising the hedges and scattered sycamore trees (*Acer pseudoplatanus*), deliberately chosen to reflect the changing seasons and to emphasize the simple character of the polder landscape.

▲ (iii) View of path

▲ (iv) View of path

4.14 Vuzenica Cemetery, Slovenia

Niko Stare

Vuzenica is a small town near Dravograd, some 10 km from the Austrian border, with a planned expansion from 3000 to 6400 population. The cemetery site of about 2 ha lies on the second terrace of the River Drava. An original design for the cemetery grounds attached to the building and the 'farewell platform', which had already been built, was rejected on the grounds of its uninteresting character, arising, perhaps, from the 'classical' formality.

The alternative approach, by the landscape architect, Niko Stare, is informal, dependent upon trees and plants to give unity and express harmony with nature. Stronger links are established with the main building and the circulation is organized on a hierarchical basis. In observance of Slovenian law, which determines that a cemetery should accommodate graves for 60 years, the implementation has been planned in stages. The first, ten-year stage has been completed; the second stage planned for thirty years, is under construction; the third has not yet been planned.

Graves are planned as single and double units linked by paths and orientated towards the cemetery building. They include graves flush with the grass, those with raised kerbs, and those with gravestones, for which the height is limited. A curved wall with niches is provided for the placing of urns.

The new 'green' approach, which has a long precedent in northern Europe, where it has links with the Romantic landscape tradition, is gaining popularity for several reasons. It reduces social distinctions (and , where appropriate, those of religion), it is more flexible than the traditional forms of cemetery, and it is cheaper. But change, in such areas of human concern, can only be effected slowly.

▼ **Figure 4.14 Vuzenica Cemetery**

(i) Plan

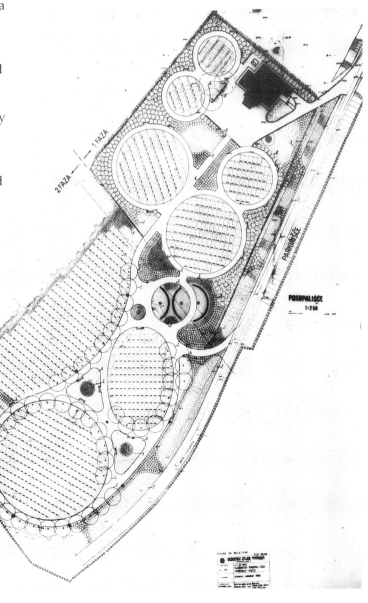

▲ (ii) General view

◀ (iii) Detail

4.15 Nove Žale Cemetery, Ljubliana, Slovenia

Marco Mušič

▲ **Figure 4.15 Nove Zale Cemetery** (i) Sketch of entrance

The new Ljubliana cemetery is an extension of that built before the war to the design of Jose Plečnik. In his design the architect chose to follow the precedent of his predecessor in adopting an architectonic rather than a naturalistic approach. This is based upon the ancient Mediterranean concept of the necropolis as an idealized and miniaturized city with streets lined with miniature temples and palaces; with 'squares', meeting places, gates and towers.

Mušič's 'City of the Dead' is surrounded by a low wall, with two small towers and impressive gates. Entrances, crossings and meeting places are marked by pavilions, pyramids and torch-like pylons. The main avenues are planted with trees; the others, lined with grave-plots, which, in accordance with Slovenian tradition, will permit either burial, the placing of ashes in urns, or their scattering

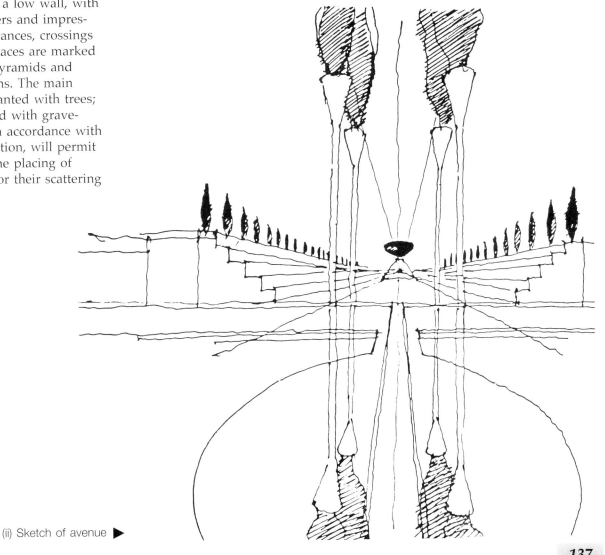

(ii) Sketch of avenue ▶

(iii) Plan ▶

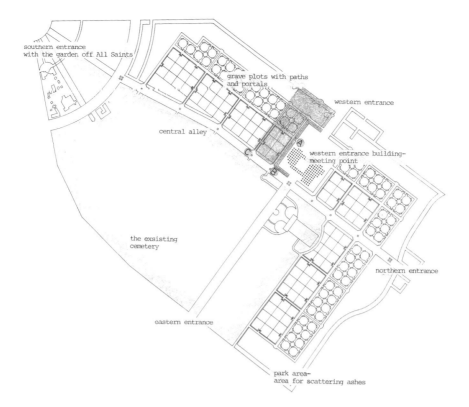

southern entrance
with the garden off All Saints

grave plots with paths
and portals

western entrance

central alley

western entrance building-
meeting point

the exsisting
cemetery

northern entrance

eastern entrance

park area-
area for scattering ashes

▼ (iv) Gate B

▲ (v) Park and area for scattering ashes

▼ (vi) Patterned concrete wall

on the ground. Historical and visual links have been established by the adoption of the line of the old Tomacevska Street as the longitudinal axis (originally with an uninterrupted view of Ljubliana Castle to the south), crossing the Pathway of Friendship and Remembrance, and linking up with the rest place Gramozna Jama.

The original proposal to use stone cladding throughout had to be abandoned on account of cost; but the situation has been turned to advantage by the careful juxtaposition of stone and concrete. Contrasts of texture have been fully exploited, both in hard materials and the climbing plants which cover them. The use of different types of stone adds subtlety of colour, and at the same time a sense of quality and permanence.

◀ (vii) Walled grave area

◀ (viii) Elevation of Gate A

▼ (ix) Detail of concrete wall

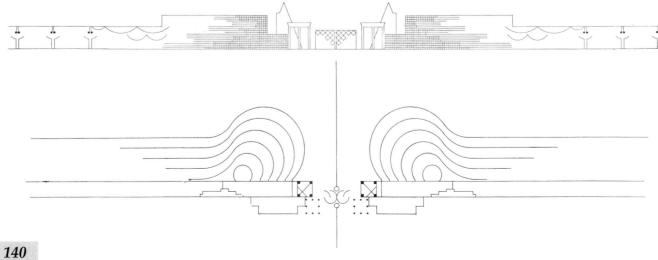

4.16 Brion Tomb, S. Vito, Treviso, Italy

Carlo Scarpa

The private cemetery for the Brion family in San Vito raises questions about the nature of architecture, of landscape and of sculpture, for it is all three. It comprises such a rich variety of forms and symbols that it cannot be disassociated with its creator – indeed, Scarpa himself is buried in a corner specially allocated just outside the wall. It takes the form of an L-shaped courtyard garden wrapped around the corner of the village necropolis. It was completed c. 1973 by Carlo Scarpa, who was given some initial advice on planting by Pietro Porcinai. The tomb of Guiseppe Brion and his wife had been placed at an angle of 45° at the corner of the L.

Outside, the unprepossessing grey concrete wall attracts only by its gate and the Scarpa signature of a stepped corner. Inside the path squeezes past a clump of cypresses to the chapel, a simple square building placed diagonally in a square pool, where there is a strong sense of the oriental. The immaculate chapel itself with its moongate entrance and the extraordinary care with which the details and materials of the surrounding paths and other elements have been dealt with, set the mood; and the water channel leads the eye towards the tomb. This comprises two concrete 'sarcophagi' simply inscribed and decorated with the step motif, leaning touchingly towards one another. They are covered by an uncompromisingly modern structure of a curved concrete canopy and four supporting beams. The canopy, which is reminiscent of those thin marble edges to Mughal tombs and pavilions, effectively presses the tomb to the earth and provides a new shape to complement the borrowed landscape of church, village and mountains beyond, when seen from the far end of the L-shaped courtyard. Here there is a large pool with water-lilies and a narrow causeway leading to a platform in the centre – another Mughal-inspired detail. But this is of concrete and it is decorated with tiles in blues, greys and greens, arranged in simple lines. Such vestiges of colour appear elsewhere – in a strip on the plain concrete back wall, where the colours are reinforced by yellow and black, and under the canopy of the tomb. These are in mosaic, of similar colours, and it has been suggested that their use is inspired by the effects of sunlight and green canal water reflected under bridges; for Scarpa is a native of Venice.

Figure 4.16 Brion Tomb
▲ (i) Detail of external corner

◀ (ii) View out from entrance area

▼ (iii) Plan

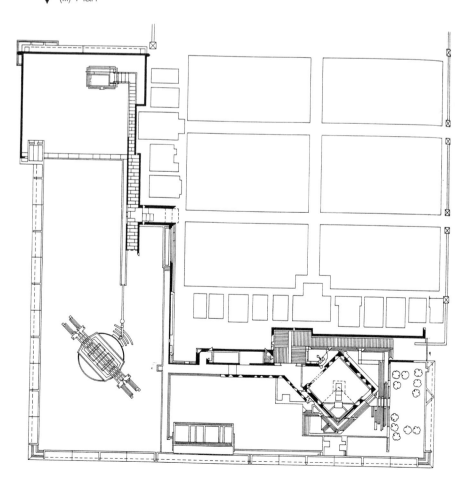

▲ (iv) General view of borrowed landscape

(v) Detail view out into
courtyard ▶

143

ART AND THE LANDSCAPE

Nature and art are too grand to go forth in pursuit of
aims; nor is it necessary that they should, for there are
relations everywhere, and relations constitute life.

(Goethe)

The decline of religion and the fragmentation of cultures
has placed artists in an equivocal position, searching
incessantly for new meanings. In many ways the arts
have blossomed, freed from the traditional constraints
imposed by society, to investigate the nature of materials and forms and to re-explore their cultural relationships. One effect of this freedom has been divisive,
separating the 'traditional' from the 'modern': exposing
both to market forces and abandoning much of the
former to the fields of restoration and memorials. The
over-flowing sculpture galleries have expanded, firstly
into courtyards, then into gardens and parks and finally
into the landscape itself. The expansion has been accompanied by new forms: areas of 'environmental sculpture'
integrated into the urban fabric, kinetic sculptures and
mechanical fountains such as that by Tingueley and
Nikki St Phalle adjoining the Centre Pompidou. Also
there is a growing realization that art and architecture,
landscape design and sculpture are linked both by
common parameters and by the urgent need to improve
the environment.

The relationship with the landscape is in one sense a
renewal of ancient ties; in another it is a unique opportunity for exploration and experimentation.
Reinterpretation of nature and landscape has been
achieved eloquently in entirely different ways in the
Land Art of Richard Long, in Christo's *Running Fence*,
and in the jewel-like sculptures made from fragments of
ice and vegetation by Andy Goldsworthy: all transient.
More permanent are the growing number of examples
of earth and rock art, continuing traditions established
in pre-historic times. In the Aexoni Quarry, the sculptress Nella Golanda has sought to 'recover the
landscape' by recreating a rock-face with cave and
cascades to give the impression that it has just been
excavated.

Sculpture gardens and parks tend to suffer from
anonymity and over-crowding. The most effective are
those stamped either with the personality of the artist or
the owner-collector; both are less susceptible to the
conflicting demands of public access and the selection
and siting of work by others. In the grounds of the Villa
di Celle, the owner, Giuliano Gori, has succeeded in
achieving a high degree of integration of a range of
different sculptures by encouraging the artists (originally mainly 'environmental artists' from North
America) to select their own sites on the conditions that
the work should be in perfect harmony both with the
site and the surrounding landscape.

The personality of the collector, Karl Heinrich Müller, is
also expressed in the Insel Hombroich, which is neither
quite art gallery, nor museum, nor sculpture park; but it
combines elements of each in expressing the theme 'Art
Parallel with Nature'. Although Monet's garden at
Giverny was a point of reference, the Insel Hombroich
dissolves the boundaries between garden and landscape,
art and nature. The landscape emphasis is on natural
regeneration, the architectural emphasis is sculptured,
the art becomes a part of life.

4.17 Aexoni Quarry, Glyfada, Attica, Greece

Nella Golanda

The project was one of a series of 'landscape recovery' projects initiated by the Municipality of Glyfada in conjunction with the Ministry of Regional Planning and Environment (1984–92).

The old quarry, an area of 6000 m², cuts a wedge into the slope of Mount Hymettus at Aexoni, the ancient city of Aexonaeon. The main feature, a sculptural concrete wall 40 m long, 10 m high and 7 m deep, is intended to dominate the site in a way that would give the visitor the impression that it has just been excavated. The right-hand end relates to the coloured rock formations, while the other end is concealed by planting. The many-faceted wall is pierced by a 'cave' and surrounded by a channel into which water cascades from several points. The surface is richly textured to express the light and shadows, and it is faced in places with pieces of marble and other stones. The area is planted with species typical of the region of Mount Hymettus; it has been formed into three levels to accommodate music recitals, theatrical performances and sculpture exhibitions. The Quarry was inaugurated in September 1992 with the celebration of the 70th birthday of the composer, Yannis Xenakis.

Figure 4.17 Aexoni Quarry

4.18 Museum fur Kunsthandwerk, Frankfurt-on-Main, Germany 1980–85

Richard Meier and Partners

The new Frankfurt museum houses a small collection of decorative arts on a site beside the River Main. The architect was faced with three problems of siting: to relate to the river, to the adjoining rococo-style mansion housing a part of the collection, and to the gardens with existing large trees. He has achieved all of these objectives with a characteristically elegant white building reminiscent of the 1930s modern style, articulated to suit the space and extending spatially over the site by means of a number of axes. These are arranged in such a way that they focus upon and pass through white concrete pergola structures, functioning rather like temples in an eighteenth-century landscape. At the crossing of the two main axes there is a fountain.

Figure 4.18 Museum fur Kunsthandwerk
View from restaurant along the main axis towards the fountain with encirling pergola catching the light against a dark background of foliage

4.19 Fattoria di Celle, Santomato di Pistoia, Italy

Giuliano Gori and Amnon Barzel

Giuliano Gori, the owner of Villa di Celle, is one of a long line of well-informed patrons of the arts who have made the Tuscan towns some of the most beautiful in the world. But he is unique in his interest in contemporary art and his dedication to its display in the grounds of the villa in Santomato di Pistoia.

The estate is one of the most important in Central Italy, both for its development and the state of preservation of the buildings. These originated in the eighteenth century (the chapel dates from 1702), but the major development of the park was in the nineteenth century, when it was designed in the Romantic style by Giovanni Gambini (c. 1845).

In 1982 Amnon Barzel was asked to collaborate in organizing a series of exhibitions, both temporary and permanent, of contemporary art. Initially the response was primarily from the 'environmental artists' of North America, but European exhibits are increasing. Unusually, artists were invited to create outdoor exhibits *in situ*; on one condition: 'that the works should be in perfect harmony with the site they have chosen and with the surrounding countryside'. Contrary to the usual practice of artists' work being sited and exhibited by others, the landscape has itself become the studio; the materials of nature a part of the whole concept. In Celle they express the *genius loci* by means of elegant structures and materials of our technology.

Figure 4.19 Fattoria di Celle
▲ (i) Entrance to villa

◀ (ii) Hill sculptures by Alice Aycock

◀ (iii) Lake sculptures
'Tema II e variazioni' by Fausto
Melotti

◀ (iv) Meadow sculptures
'Katarsis' by Magdalena
Abakanowic

148

4.20 Insel Hombroich, Neuss, Düsseldorf, Germany

Bernhardt Korte: Erwin Heerich

The art collector Karl Heinrich Müller bought the Düsseldorf site in 1984 with the intention of leaving his collection to the public. The country house of the de Weerth family from Wuppertal had been planned with a formal garden in 1820, which has subsequently disappeared, and in 1900 the Erft stream was diverted to surround the whole estate. After renovating 'the Pink House' in which he installed his collection of watercolours, Müller turned his attention to the grounds comprising an overgrown woodland garden with farm buildings and a large expanse of derelict water-meadows, covering some 3 ha (by 1992 this area had been increased to more than 8 ha).

Müller invited the agronomist and teacher Bernhardt Korte to join the team of planners, designers and artists who would contribute to the creation of 'the island'. The theme was to be 'Art Parallel with Nature'; the content, a number of pavilions containing works of art, others to be 'seen' as works of 'art' in themselves, sculptures and objects in the landscape. A point of reference was to be Monet's garden at Giverny, but clearly both the site and the wide-ranging tastes of the owner pointed to something very different.

The simple geometric pavilions by Erwin Heerich (a sculptor turned architect) can be seen as 'walk-in

Figure 4.20 Insel Hombroich Neuss

◄ (i) General view

◄ (ii) General view

sculptures' as well as buildings, and indeed many of them are simply enclosures of space. The reference to de Stijl and the Bauhaus are confirmed by a visit to the 'museum' buildings. But the image of a museum has been carefully avoided, and the collection includes everything from ancient pottery to modern furniture. The sculptor, Anatol Herzfeld, who is also a policeman, works with trees and flowers, and he has made a landscape with blocks of stone and a house of lead. The painter, Gotthard Graubner, uses the colours of flowers and foliage as his inspiration.

The aims of the landscape architect were twofold: firstly to respect the genius of the place, contributing with the other participants, to the development of a special place in which art and nature are irrevocably linked. Secondly to develop particular areas in particular ways. The exist-ing landscape of the water-meadows was a landscape that had been despoiled by the opencast mining of coal, but soil tests revealed 40 cm of humus at 2 m depth, containing pollen grains from numerous species. The alignment and banks of the stream were changed, ponds created and White Willows, Black Poplars and ash trees planted to provide a structure for floral regen-eration. The neglected woodland became the subject of management plans, and certain areas selected for detailed small-scale planting. This includes the restora-tion of traces of the old gardens, such as the small box-hedged formal garden, areas of herbaceous plants and ornamental shrubs and trees.

The result is a developing landscape that is neither quite garden, nor park, nor is it a museum or sculpture garden; it combines qualities of all of these in a unique way.

◀ (iii) View of sculpture pavilion

◀ (iv) Detail

Bibliography and references

Alexander, C. (1964)	*Notes on the Synthesis of Form*, Oxford University Press
Alexander, C. (1977)	*A Pattern Language*, Oxford University Press
Andersson, T. (1993)	'Erik Glemme and the Stockholm Park System', *Modern Landscape Architecture* (M. Treib, ed.), MIT
Appleton, J. (1986)	*The Experience of Landscape*, John Wiley
Appleton, J. (Ed.) (1980)	*The Aesthetics of Landscape*, University of Hull
Appleyard, D., Lynch, K. and Myer, J.R. (1964)	*A View from the Road*, MIT
Arkell, V.T.J. (1978)	*Britain Transformed*, Penguin Education
Arnheim, R. (1968)	'Gestalt Psychology and Artistic Form', *Aspects of Form* (L.L. Whyte, ed.), Lund Humphries
Arnheim, R. (1974)	*Art and Visual Perception*, University of California
Arvill, R. (1967)	*Man and Environment*, Penguin
Attenborough, D. (1979)	*Life on Earth*, BBC
Attenborough, D. (1990)	*The Living Planet*, BBC
Bacon, E.N. (1967)	*Design of Cities*, Thames & Hudson
Bartha, S. (1984)	*Ecological Design*, Association for Ecological Design
Bell, C. and R. (1969)	*City Fathers*, Barrie Cresset
Berger, J. (1972)	*Ways of Seeing*, BBC
Bernatzky, A. (1969)	*The Performance and Value of Trees*
Bertram, A. (1939)	*Design*, Penguin
Blackett, H. (1986)	'Cemeteries', *Oxford Companion to Gardens*, Oxford University Press
Bourassia, S.C. (1991)	*The Aesthetics of Landscape*, Belhaven Press
Bramwell, A. (1990)	*Ecology in the 20th Century*, Yale
Bronowski, J. (1981)	*The Ascent of Man*, BBC
Brown, J. (1982)	*The Everywhere Landscape*, Wildwood House
Burke, E. (1767)	*Enquiries into the Origin of Our Ideas of the Sublime and Beautiful*, London
Carter Goode, L. (1982)	*Humphry Repton*, V & A Museum
Chevreul, M.E. (1881)	*The Principles of Harmony and Contrast of Colours and their Application to the Arts*, George Bell
Ching, F.D.K. (1979)	*Architecture: Form, Space & Order*, Van Nostrand Reinhold
Chisholm, A. (1971)	*Philosophers of the Earth*, London
Clark, K. (1961)	*Landscape into Art*, Penguin
Clegg, F. (1989)	'Cemeteries for the Living', *Landscape Design* (No. 184)
Colvin, B. (1948)	*Land and Landscape*, John Murray
Le Corbusier, (1970)	*Towards a New Architecture*, Architectural Press
Crook, J.M. (1987)	*The Dilemma of Style*, John Murray

Crowe, S. (1956)	*Tomorrow's Landscape*, Architectural Press
Crowe, S. (1958)	*The Landscape of Power*, Architectural Press
Crowe, S. (1966)	*Forestry in the Landscape*, Forestry Commission
Cullen, G. (1971)	*Townscape*, Architectural Press
Dawkins, R. (1986)	*The Blind Watchmaker*, Longman
Dixon-Hunt, J. (1993)	'The Dialogue of Modern Landscape Architecture with its Past', *Modern Landscape Architecture* (M. Treib, ed.), MIT
Domus (1992)	'Espais Publics a Barcelona', No. 738, May
Droscher, V.B. (1971)	*The Magic of the Senses*, W.H. Allen/Panther
Edelman, G. (1992)	*Bright Air, Brilliant Fire*, Harper Collins/Penguin
Elliot, B. (1986)	*Victorian Gardens*, Batsford
Fairbrother, N. (1972)	*New Lives, New Landscapes*, Penguin
Fairbrother, N. (1974)	*The Nature of Landscape Design*, Architectural Press
Fieldhouse, K. and Harvey, S. (1992)	*Landscape Design: An International Survey*, Laurence King
von Franz, M.L. (1978)	*Time*, Thames & Hudson
Fraser-Darling, F. (1970)	*Wilderness and Plenty*, BBC/Ballantyne Books
Freeman, W.H. and Bracegirdle, B. (1971)	*An Atlas of Invertebrate Structure*, Heinemann
von Frisch, K. (1975)	*Animal Architecture*, Hutchinson
Fry, E.M. (1969)	*Art in a Machine Age*, Methuen
Gibson, J.J. (1979)	*The Perception of the Visual World*, Greenwood
Gimpel, J. (1961)	*The Cathedral Builders*, Evergreen
Gimpel, J. (1988)	*The Medieval Machine*, Pimlico
Girouard, M. (1985)	*Cities & People*, Yale
Gleick, J. (1988)	*Chaos*, Heinemann
Goldsmith, E. (1992)	*The Way: an Ecological World View*, Rider
Gombrich, E.H. (1984)	*The Sense of Order*, Phaidon
Goode, P. (1986)	'Public Parks', *Oxford Companion to Gardens*, Oxford University Press
Gregory, R.L. and Gombrich, E.H. (1980)	*Illusion in Nature & Art*, Duckworth
Grigson, G. (1971)	*Britain Observed*, Phaidon
Grillo, (1960)	*Form, Function & Design*, Dover
Guccione, B. (1990)	*Paesaggio Parchi Giardini*, Aquarius Editrice/Firenz
Hall, E. (1969)	*The Hidden Dimension*
Hancocks, D. (1971)	*Animals and Architecture*, Evelyn
Hatje, G. (Ed) (1965)	*Encyclopaedia of Modern Architecture*, Thames & Hudson
Hawkes, J. (1959)	*A Land*, Penguin
Hazlehurst, H. (1980)	*Gardens of Illusion*, Vanderbilt University Press
Hobhouse, P. (1985)	*Colour in your Garden*, Collins
Hogarth, W. (1753)	*The Analysis of Beauty*, London
Holden, R. (1991)	'Barcelona Revitalized', *Landscape Architecture*, Jan/Feb
Holden, R. and Turner, T. (1990)	Parks in Peril, *Building Design*, 4 May
Hoskins, W.G. (1976)	*English Landscapes*, BBC
Hoskins, W.G. (1978)	*One Man's England*, BBC
Hoskins, W.G. (1979)	*The Making of the English Landscape*, Penguin
Howel-Evans, D. (1992)	'Going for Gold', *Building Design*, 24 July
Humphrey, N. (1976)	'The Colour Currency of Nature', *Colour for Architecture* (T. Porter and B. Mikellides, eds), Studio Vista
Hunter, J.M. (1985)	*Land into Landscape*, George Godwin
International Federation of Landscape Architects (1981)	*IFLA Education Report*
Jacobs, J. (1964)	*The Death and Life of the Great American Cities*, Penguin
Jellicoe, G.A. (1970)	*Studies in Landscape Design* Vols. 1, 2 & 3, Oxford University Press
Jellicoe, G. and S. (1975)	*The Landscape of Man*, Thames & Hudson
Jellicoe, G.A. Goode, P. and Lancaster, M.L. (1986)	*The Oxford Companion to Gardens*, Oxford University Press
Jencks, C. (1985)	*Modern Movements in Architecture*, Penguin
Jencks, C. (Ed) (1980)	*Signs, Symbols and Architecture* (G. Broadbent, ed.), Wiley
Jencks, C. (1992)	'Leap frogging the Cultural Pyramid', *Guardian*, 16 January

152

Johnson, H. (1984)   *The Principles of Gardening*, Mitchell Beazley

Johnston, R.S. (1991)   *Scholar Gardens of China*, Cambridge University Press

Joyce, D. (ed) (1989)   *Garden Styles: Gardens of the 20th century*, Pyramid

Jung, C.G. (1964)   *Man and his symbols*, Aldis

Kassler, E.B. (1964)   *Modern Gardens and the Landscape*, Museum of Modern Art.

Kennedy, P. (1993)   *Preparing for the Twenty-first Century*, Harper Collins

Keswick, M. (1978)   *The Chinese Garden*, Academy Editions

Kidder Smith, G.E. (1954)   *Italy Builds*, Architectural Press

Knevett, C. (1985)   *Space on Earth*, Thames/Methuen

Koestler, A. (1969)   *Act of Creation* Pan

Lancaster, M. (1984)   *Britain in View: colour and the landscape*, Quiller Press

Lancaster, M. (1987)   'Painting, Colour and the Landscape' *Landscape Design* No. 168, August

Lancaster, M. (1987)   'Colour for Planners', *The Planner*, July

Lancaster, M. (1988)   'The Englishness of English Gardens', *The Garden*, April

Lancaster, M. (1989)   'Colour and Plants' *Landscape Design* No. 179, April

Laurie, M. (1976)   *An Introduction to Landscape Architecture*, Pitman

Leach, E. (1970)   *Len-Strauss*, Fontana

Lovelock, J. (1989)   *The Ages of Gaia: a biography of our living earth*, Oxford University Press

Lovelock, J. (1979)   *A New Look at Earth*, Oxford University Press

Lowenthal, D. (1985)   *The Past is a Foreign Country*

Lyall, S. (1991)   *Designing the New Landscape*, Thames & Hudson

Lynch, K. (1965)   *The Image of the City*, MIT

Lynch, K. (1971)   *Site Planning*, MIT

Lynch, K. (1972)   *What time is this place?* MIT

Malthus, T. (1798)   *Population*

Mangham, S. (1944)   *Earth's Green Mantle*, English Universities Press

Marais, E. (1973)   *The Soul of the White Ant*, Penguin

Martienssen, H. (1976)   *The Shapes of Structure*, Oxford University Press

McHarg, I. (1971)   *Design with Nature*, Natural History Press

McKibbern, B. (1990)   *The End of Nature*, Viking

Michaels and Ricks, C. (eds) (1980)   *The State of the Language*, University of California

Michell, J. (1975)   *The Earth Spirit*, Thames & Hudson

Moore, C.W., Mithcell, W.J.
  and Turnbull, W. Jr. (1989)   *The Poetics of Gardens*, MIT

Muir, R. (1981)   *The English Village*, Thames & Hudson

Mumford, D. (1966)   *The City in History*, Penguin

Muschenheim, W. (1965)   *Elements of the Art of Architecture*, Thames & Hudson

Muthesius, H. (1987)   *The English House* (1904/5/8-11), BSP Professional

Nasr, S.H. (1976)   *Islamic Science*, World of Islam

Nicholson, M. (1972)   *The Environmental Revolution*, Penguin

Norberg-Schulz, C. (1971)   *Existence, Space and Architecture*, Studio Vista

Norberg-Schulz, C. (1980)   *Genius Loci: towards a phenomenonology of architecture*, Academic Ed.

North, R. (1990)   'Why Man Can Never Kill Nature', *Independent*, 2 January

Nuttgens, P. (1972)   *The Landscape of Ideas*, Faber & Faber

Nuttgens, P. (1983)   *The Story of Architecture*, Phaidon

Oliver, P. (1969)   *Shelter & Society*, Barrie & Jenkins

Papanek, V. (1985)   *Design for the Real World*, Thames & Hudson

Pearson, D. (1989)   *The Natural House Book*, Conran/Octopus

Perin, C. (1972)   *With Man in Mind*, MIT

Pevsner, N. (1945)   *An Outline of European Architecture*, Penguin

Pevsner, N. (1964)   *Pioneers of Modern Design*, Penguin

Pevsner, N. (1986)   *The Sources of Modern Architecture and Design*, Thames & Hudson

Pikionis, D. (1935)   *A Sentimental Topography*, Architectural Association

Popper, K. (1979)   *Objective Knowledge*, Oxford University Press

Porritt, J. (1990)   *Where on Earth are we Going*, BBC

Porter, T. and Mikellides, B. (1976)   *Colour for Architecture*, Studio Vista

Porter, T. (1982)   *Colour Outside*, Architectural Press

Porter, T. and Goodman (1988) *Designer Primer*

Prime, R. (1992) *Hinduism and Ecology*, Cassell

Pye, D. (1969) *The Nature of Design*, Studio Vista

Pye, D. (1971) *The Nature and Art of Workmanship*, Studio Vista

Rasmusson, S.E. (1960) *London the Unique City*, Penguin

Rawson, P. and Legeza, L. (eds) (1973) *Tao: the Chinese philosophy of time and change*, Thames & Hudson

Read, H. (1958) *Education through Art*, Faber & Faber

Richards, J.M. and de Maré, E. (1958) *The Functional Tradition*, Architectural Press

Rossbach, S. (1983) *Feng Shui*, Oxford University Press

Rudofsky, B. (1964) *Architecture without Architects*, Doubleday

Ruff, A. (1986) 'Ecology and Gardens', *Oxford Companion to Gardens*, Oxford University Press

den Ruijter, M. (1987) Functional Festivity: Floriade 1992, *Landscape Design*, No. 167, June

Santayana, G. (1961) *The Sense of Beauty*, Cambridge University Press

de Sausmarez, M. (1967) *Basic Design: the dynamics of visual form*, Studio Vista

Schumacher, F. (1973) *Small is Beautiful*, Blond & Briggs/Abacus

Schwartz, W. (1992) 'Building a church for Gaia', *Guardian*, 5 September

Scully, V. (1988) *Architecture: the natural and the man-made, in Denatured Visions*

Scully, V. (1991) *De-natured Visions* (S. Wrede and W.H. Adams, eds), Museum of Modern Art

Sharp, T. (1953) *The Anatomy of the Village*, Penguin

Shepheard, P. (1954) *Modern Gardens*, Architectural Press

Silver, N. (1980) 'Architect Talk', *The State of the Language* (L. Michaels and C. Ricks, eds), University of California

Simonds, J.O. (1961) *Landscape Architecture*, Iliffe

Smith, P. (1976) 'The Dialectics of Colour', *Colour for Architecture* (T. Porter and B. Mikellides, eds)

Snow, C.P. (1959) *The Two Cultures*, BBC

Stevens, P.S. (1976) *Patterns in Nature*, Little, Brown & Co

Stilgoe, R. (1982) *Common Landscapes of America 1580—1845*, Yale University Press

Storr, A. (1972) *The Dynamics of Creation*, Secker & Warburg

Storr, A. (1988) *The School of Geniuses*, Andre Deutsch

Strachan, W.J. (1984) *Open Air Sculpture in Britain*, Zwemmar/Tate Gallery

Stroud, D. (1975) *Capability Brown*, Faber

Sudjic, D. (1990) 'Homage to Catalonian Planning', *Guardian*, 16 July

Summerson, J. (1962) *Georgian London*, Penguin

Tandy, C. (1975) *Landscape of Industry*, Leonard Hill

Taverne, E. and Wagenaar, C. (1992) *Colour of the City*, V & K Publishing

Taylor, N. (1973) *The Village in the City*, Temple Smith

Thomas, L. (1979) *The Lives of a Cell*, Alan Lane

Thompson, J. D'A. (1961) *On Growth and Form*, Cambridge

Tischler, W.H. (Ed) (1989) *American Landscape Architecture: designers and places*, Preservation Press

Tortora and Agnostakos (1984) *Principles of Anatomy and Physiology*, Harper International

Treib, M. (ed) (1933) *Modern Landscape Architecture: a critical review*, MIT

Tucker, W. (1981) *The Language of Sculpture*, Thames & Hudson

Tunnard, C. (1948) *Gardens in the Modern Landscape*, Architectural Press

Turan, M. (ed) (1990) *Vernacular Architecture*, Avebury

Turner, T. (1986) *English Garden Design: history and styles since 1650*, Antique Collectors' Club

Turner, T. (1987) *Landscape Planning*, Hutchinson

Tzonis, A. and Lefaivre, L. (1992) *Architecture in Europe since 1968*, Thames & Hudson

Venturi, R. (1977) *Complexity and Contradiction in Architecture*, Museum of Modern Art

Vitruvius, (translated by Morgan, M.H.) (1960) *The Ten Books on Architecture*, Dover

Waddington, C.H. (1968) 'The character of biological form', *Aspects of Form* (L.L. Whyte, ed.), Lund Humphries

Wagenaar, C. (ed) (1982) *The Colour of the City*, V & K Publishing

154

Walmsley, A. (1975) *Made Landscapes from Prehistory to the Present*

Watson, L. (1984) *Heaven's Breath*, Hodder & Stoughton

Watts (1993) *Independent*, 31 August

Whyte, L.L. (ed) (1968) *Aspects of Form*, Lund Humphries

Woodward, C. (1992) *The Buildings of Europe*, Barcelona

Wrede, S. and Adams, W.H. (eds) (1991) *Denatured Visions: landscape and culture in the twentieth century*, Museum of Modern Art

Figure credits

Jette Abel	3.2 (iii)
Ajuntament de Barcelona	3.7 (vii), (viii), (ix), (x)
G. Akdogan	4.6 (ii), (iii)
L'Anton	3.6 (v)
Architecture (September 1992)	3.6 (vi) (a)
Arquitectura Revista	3.7 (ii), (v)
Arup Associates	2.13 (i)–(iii); 2.14 (ii); 3.11 (i)
Ashmolean Museum	4.1 (i)
Karen Attwell	3.2 (ii); Blomsterhaven
Gae Aulenti	4.3 (iii)
Louise Baxter	Fawley Power Station (ii)
Brioschi, Bellinzona	2.10 (ii); 2.11 (ii)–(iv); 2.12 (ii), (iii)
Brodsky	3.7 (iv)
Karl D. Bühler/Comet Photo AG	3.9 (i)–(iii)
Paolo Bürgi	2.10 (i); 2.11 (i); 2.12 (i)
Edward Butcher	Fawley Power Station (i)
Martin Charles	2.14 (iii)
City of Luxembourg	3.8 (i)
City of Turku	2.2 (i)
Jeremy Cockayne	3.11 (iii)
Commission for New Towns	3.3 (i)
Peter Cook	3.11 (ii)
Jenny Cox	3.4 (ii)
Dufresne	3.6 (i), (ii), (vi), (vii)
Morton Falmer-Nielsen	4.12 (i)
Faulks, Perry, Culley and Rech	Stanstead Airport (i), (ii)
Floriade	2.9 (i)
Garten u. Landschaft	2.5 (i); 2.7 (i)
Christophe Girot	3.6 (iii), (iv)
Frans Grumner/Etienne van Sloun	3.10 (i)–(iii)
Grzimek	2.4 (iii)
Biagio Guccione	4.2; 4.4; 4.19 (i)–(iv)
Weier de Haas	3.8 (ii)
IGA Stuttgart	2.8 (i), (ii)
D. Kalapodas	4.11 (i), (ii) (a), (b)
H.C. Koningen	Thijssepark
Michael Lancaster	2.4 (i), (iv)–(vi); 3.1 (ii); 3.2 (v); 3.4 (i), (iii); 3.6 (iv); 4.12 (ii)–(v); 4.16 (i), (ii), (iv), (v); 4.18; 4.20 (i)–(iv); Vaerebroparken; Great Linford, Milton Keynes; Staatsgalerie

Index